How Are Online Activities Affecting Society?

Bonnie Szumski and Jill Karson

INCONTROVERSY

ReferencePoint Press®

San Diego, CA

Printed in the United States

For more information, contact:
ReferencePoint Press, Inc.
PO Box 27779
San Diego, CA 92198
www. ReferencePointPress.com

Photo Credits:
Cover: iStockphoto.com
AP Images: 63
© Alessandro Della Bella/Keystone/Corbis: 14
© Oliver Berg/dpa/Corbis: 49
© Julio Cortez/AP/Corbis: 71
© Aristide Econonpoulos/Star Ledger/Corbis: 55
© Rick Friedman/Corbis: 21
Elisa Haberer: 41
© Ron Haviv/VII/Corbis: 75
© Tim Shaffer/Reuters/Corbis: 12
© Paul Sakuma/AP/Corbis: 7
Thinkstock Images: 29, 34
© Julian Winslow/ableimages/Corbis: 58

LIBRARY OF CONGRESS CATALOGING-IN-PUBLICATION DATA

Szumski, Bonnie, 1958–
How are online activities affecting society? / by Bonnie Szumski and Jill Karson.
pages cm. -- (In controversy)
Audience: Grade 9 to 12
Includes bibliographical references and index.
ISBN-13: 978-1-60152-546-8 (hardback)
ISBN-10: 1-60152-546-X (hardback)
1. Online social networks--Juvenile literature. 2. Internet--History--Juvenile literature. I. Karson, Jill. II. Title.
HM742.S98 2013
006.7'54--dc23

2013017164

Contents

Foreword

In 2008, as the US economy and economies worldwide were falling into the worst recession since the Great Depression, most Americans had difficulty comprehending the complexity, magnitude, and scope of what was happening. As is often the case with a complex, controversial issue such as this historic global economic recession, looking at the problem as a whole can be overwhelming and often does not lead to understanding. One way to better comprehend such a large issue or event is to break it into smaller parts. The intricacies of global economic recession may be difficult to understand, but one can gain insight by instead beginning with an individual contributing factor, such as the real estate market. When examined through a narrower lens, complex issues become clearer and easier to evaluate.

This is the idea behind ReferencePoint Press's *In Controversy* series. The series examines the complex, controversial issues of the day by breaking them into smaller pieces. Rather than looking at the stem cell research debate as a whole, a title would examine an important aspect of the debate such as *Is Stem Cell Research Necessary?* or *Is Embryonic Stem Cell Research Ethical?* By studying the central issues of the debate individually, researchers gain a more solid and focused understanding of the topic as a whole.

Each book in the series provides a clear, insightful discussion of the issues, integrating facts and a variety of contrasting opinions for a solid, balanced perspective. Personal accounts and direct quotes from academic and professional experts, advocacy groups, politicians, and others enhance the narrative. Sidebars add depth to the discussion by expanding on important ideas and events. For quick reference, a list of key facts concludes every chapter. Source notes, an annotated organizations list, bibliography, and index provide student researchers with additional tools for papers and class discussion.

The *In Controversy* series also challenges students to think critically about issues, to improve their problem-solving skills, and to sharpen their ability to form educated opinions. As President Barack Obama stated in a March 2009 speech, success in the twenty-first century will not be measurable merely by students' ability to "fill in a bubble on a test but whether they possess 21st century skills like problem-solving and critical thinking and entrepreneurship and creativity." Those who possess these skills will have a strong foundation for whatever lies ahead.

No one can know for certain what sort of world awaits today's students. What we can assume, however, is that those who are inquisitive about a wide range of issues; open-minded to divergent views; aware of bias and opinion; and able to reason, reflect, and reconsider will be best prepared for the future. As the international development organization Oxfam notes, "Today's young people will grow up to be the citizens of the future: but what that future holds for them is uncertain. We can be quite confident, however, that they will be faced with decisions about a wide range of issues on which people have differing, contradictory views. If they are to develop as global citizens all young people should have the opportunity to engage with these controversial issues."

In Controversy helps today's students better prepare for tomorrow. An understanding of the complex issues that drive our world and the ability to think critically about them are essential components of contributing, competing, and succeeding in the twenty-first century.

The Fear of Invention

The online world is everywhere; it touches nearly every aspect of daily life. A person might start the day with an alarm chirping from a cell phone, have breakfast while reading a newspaper on a digital tablet, drive to an appointment with the help of a GPS device, use a computer and the Internet at work, and check traffic on a cell phone app before leaving the office. Once at home, that same person might enjoy on-demand programming or download a movie, play an online game, or catch up with friends on a social network. Even in areas with less access to technology, the playing field is leveled by schools and jobs that provide such devices. As writer Richard Conniff says:

> Our technology is as nebulous as "the cloud," that Web-based limbo where our digital thoughts increasingly go to spend eternity. It's as liquid as the chemical contaminants our infants suck down with their mothers' milk and as ubiquitous as the genetically modified crops in our gas tanks and on our dinner plates. Technology is everywhere, knows all our thoughts and, in the words of the technology utopian Kevin Kelly, is even "a divine phenomenon that is a reflection of God." Who are we to resist?[1]

"Technology is everywhere, knows all our thoughts and, in the words of the technology utopian Kevin Kelly, is even 'a divine phenomenon that is a reflection of God.' Who are we to resist?"[1]

— Writer Richard Conniff.

Scrambling to Understand

As people become more dependent on the devices that are part of this second industrial revolution, commentators, scientists, and governments are scrambling to understand the impact such devices have on society. The Swiss scientist Conrad Gessner once described how the modern world overwhelmed people with data and said that this overabundance was both "confusing and harmful"[2] to the mind. Gessner was actually writing in 1565, and his subject was the printing press. It seems that for as long as people have been inventing, they have feared the impact of such inventions.

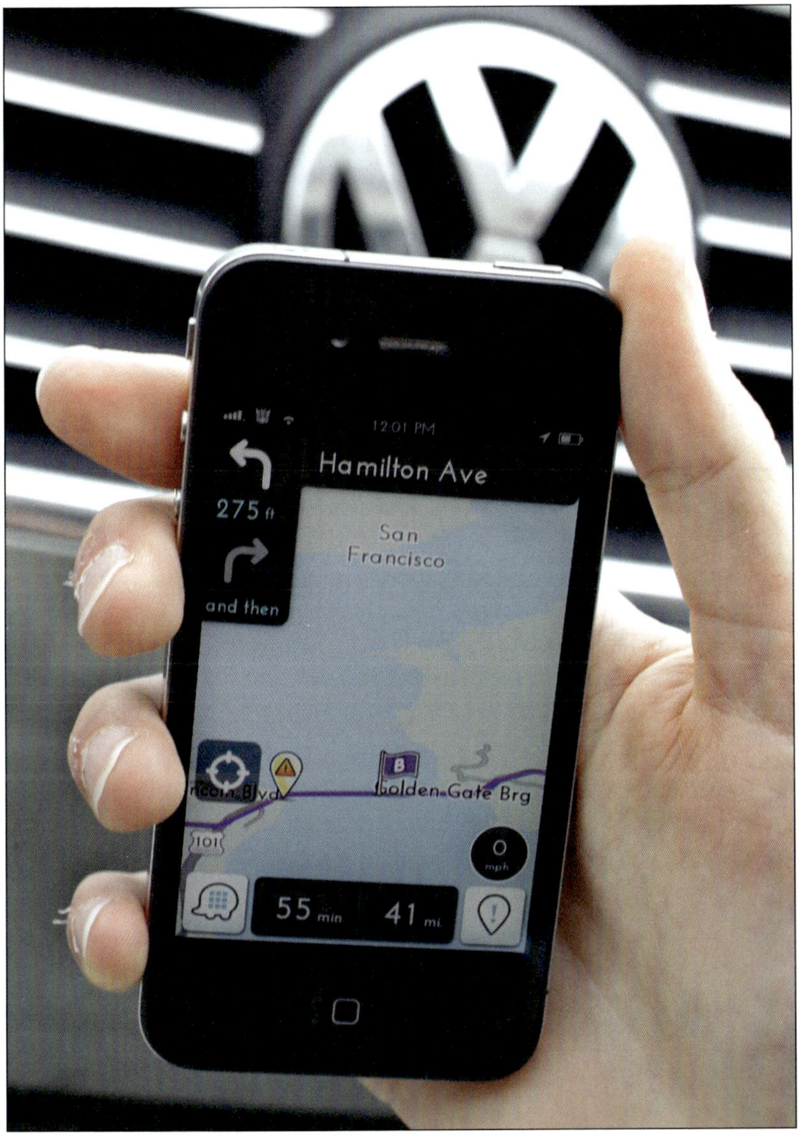

Smartphones with GPS apps that provide maps, navigation help, and traffic updates are becoming increasingly common, as are many other online activities. No longer a novelty, online access has become an essential part of daily life for people around the world.

Concerns about new and different changes bringing about unwanted behaviors have parallels even further back in time. The ancient Greek philosopher Socrates once complained about children learning how to write in a world where previously only an oral tradition transmitted knowledge. Socrates thought that writing would "create forgetfulness in the learners' souls, because they will not use their memories."[3] Such warnings are strikingly similar to concerns being expressed today about the impact of Internet use on the brain. One 2011 report of a study by Chinese scientists noted that people's brains are changing due to use of the Internet—specifically the brain's ability to pay attention for long periods and to retain information. According to the report, the brains of Internet users had atrophied—shrinking 10 to 20 percent—in areas responsible for "processing of speech, memory, motor control, emotion, sensory, and other information."[4]

Echoes from the Past

What is surprising is how these opinions from the past—almost from the dawn of literacy—echo our own, even in the language that is used. The Scottish philosopher and essayist Thomas Carlyle, writing in 1829, argued that the technology of the Industrial Revolution was causing a "mighty change" in people's "modes of thought and feeling."[5]

Should today's technology users take comfort in knowing that such fears have been a constant in human experience? Technology is most certainly changing people's habits and how they accomplish everyday tasks. But whether it is changing human nature remains open to debate and possibly even to the judgment of future generations.

Facts

- The global market for tablet computers surged 78.4 percent in 2012, with 128 million of the devices shipped, according to a survey by the research firm IDC.
- According to the Pew Internet & American Life Project, as of December 2012, 87 percent of American adults had a cell phone and 45 percent of American adults had a smartphone.
- The US consumer spends an average of 2 hours and 38 minutes per day on smartphones and tablets, with 80 percent of that time (2 hours and 7 minutes) spent using apps, the app analytics company, Flurry, reported in April 2013.
- According to the website Internetworldstats.com, as of June 2012 Asia had more Internet users than any other region, followed by Europe and North America.
- Focus group discussions conducted by the Pew Internet & American Life Project for the May 2013 Teens, Social Media, and Privacy survey show that teens have waning enthusiasm for Facebook because of the growing adult presence, excessive sharing of personal information, and stressful drama, but they keep using it because participation is an important part of teenage socializing.

What Led to the Debate over How Online Activities Affect Society?

The Internet is a complex web of networks that links millions of computing devices worldwide. The Internet originated in the early 1970s when the US Department of Defense developed ARPANET. This ancestor of the Internet was thought to have a military application only, linking wide-ranging personnel and operations. However, because ARPANET offered an unprecedented communication medium and wildly improved flow of information, it was soon adopted for social uses. William Davidow, author of *Overconnected: The Promise and Threat of the Internet*, calls the Internet "the most effective connection machine in the history of humankind."[6] He explains:

> Since its unprepossessing origins nearly four decades ago as an academic experiment, the Internet has become the medium in which much of advanced global society now functions. And it caught on quickly—from 10 million users in 1995 to an estimated 1.9 billion in 2010. Its reach

was broad: it spanned the world and affected people in the most developed and the least developed countries. It revolutionized communication. It was fast, cheap, reliable, and easy to use.[7]

New Ways to Connect

Though its adoption was fast growing, the first attempts at the Internet did not resemble the quick and easy version that is used today. One of the Internet's early developers, British scientist Tim Berners-Lee, created a system to post web pages—basically, linked documents stored on the Internet. His intent was to help him remember material he had accessed and to make that material available to others in his field of physics. His early attempts, made in the 1980s, soon spread to the general population.

The Internet's development became much more rapid when, in 1991, President George H.W. Bush signed into law the High Performance Computing and Communication Act. This bill, written and introduced by Tennessee senator Al Gore, supported research and development of the networking infrastructure that would lead to an information superhighway. Part of the development, for example, led to the first web browser, which allowed people to use links to move back and forth between pages by simply clicking on images and words. Web browsers made the Internet much more accessible to ordinary people, who in turn began buying home computers in greater numbers. With the growth and spread of this new technology, the Internet took off with lightning speed: In 1994, for example, 634 websites existed on the Internet. By 2012, that number was well over 200 million.

These technologies led to other ways people could connect online—transforming almost all areas of human activity. One of the most transformative was personal online publishing and communication. Bulletin board systems, discussion forums, and other public forums were the forerunners of modern chat groups and online communications. For the first time, users could communicate with thousands of others almost instantly. In 1994, for instance, Justin Hall, nineteen, started the first blog with a wide following—a web-based diary called *Links to the Underground*. At

The online shopping giant Amazon (one of its warehouses is pictured) became a model for millions of other businesses and transformed how people shop. Most businesses now have some sort of online presence—and many have opted for online-only transactions.

the time, his raw, personal musings and the intimate details of his life were considered racy and shocking—but were hugely popular. Today such self-revelations are considered mainstream. In December 2004 the *New York Times* called Hall the "founding father"[8] of personal blogging.

Another transformation occurred in online shopping and product ratings. Retailers began to see a future for selling products online. Every retail business created an online presence; some skipped a brick-and-mortar business altogether to go online from the start. The largest online retailer to date, Amazon, launched in 1995 and set a standard that would be a model for millions of others.

People adapted to innovations almost as soon as they were developed. Internet developers grew quickly to accommodate demand. In 1998 Larry Page and Sergey Brin founded the search engine Google to "organize the world's information and make it universally accessible and useful,"[9] according to Google's mission statement. Indeed, Google made searching the Internet accessible to all, setting the standard for searching the web. Soon, multitudes of people—retailers, educators, politicians, scientists, and others—were developing websites for users around the globe to access. Commenting on this universal adoption of the Internet, in 1996 President Bill Clinton said, "When I took office [in 1993], only high energy physicists had ever heard of what is called the World Wide Web. . . . Now even my cat has its own page."[10]

Blogging

Though Internet-savvy individuals such as Hall already understood the benefits of blogging, the first true blogging service, called Blogger, launched in 1999. Blogger provided a format so easy to use that virtually anyone could start his or her own blog. As testament, when terrorists attacked the World Trade Center in New York City in 2001, Blogger provided a forum for thousands of individuals' expressions of grief, public outcry, and shared pain. It was the first time so many people had reacted to a national event by using the web. Now, people's opinions of news events are sometimes considered as important as the original media reports. This form of media reporting and opinion, sometimes called citizen journalism, was the latest way for the person in the street to have his or her opinion heard.

Though blogging initially developed as a rather static forum for people to publish their own writings and personal thoughts, it quickly shifted to a continually updated communication device. According to Marcia Clemmitt in the *CQ Researcher*, online "content and applications are no longer created and published by individuals, but instead are continuously modified by all users in a participatory and collaborative fashion."[11] The publication goes on to give examples such as YouTube posters creating an online archive of a musician's live and electronic performances. Some blogs are dedicated to sifting through and curating the best reporting on a particular news event so that like-minded people can come to the blog to read about the event and comment on the news with others who agree with them.

The Advent of Social Networking

In 2003 the launch of MySpace created the concept of online social networking. Facebook, founded the following year, soon became the most popular social network in the world. By early 2013 Facebook had more than a billion users worldwide. The verb *to Facebook* is now common lexicon among Americans. The site's easy-to-use format, as well as the ability to maintain and find new "friends" continuously and keep up with them in the virtual world, has made it the most popular site of its kind. Facebook membership continues to grow. The average user contributes ninety pieces of content to the site each month. And Facebook is not just a US phenomenon; 70 percent of its users are outside the United States.

While content sharing became a standard of social networking, YouTube made sharing videos easy and ubiquitous. The video-sharing site uploaded its first video in April 2005 with Jawed Karim, one of the founders, featured in the video *Me at the Zoo*. YouTube became so popular that Google purchased the site for $1.65 billion one year later. In 2013 YouTube continued to be a go-to site for millions. Every minute, users upload twenty-

Although Facebook was not the first social networking site, it is the world's most popular such site. Through Facebook and other social networking sites, people can easily connect with others who share their interests, as well as stay in touch with friends and relatives.

four hours' worth of video to YouTube. As one YouTube company representative explained, "A good way to understand this is if all three major U.S. TV networks [NBC, CBS, and ABC] had been broadcasting for 24 hours a day, seven days a week, for 60 years, they still wouldn't equal the amount of content uploaded to YouTube in under 60 days."[12]

YouTube's sheer diversity is remarkable. While still a popular one-stop shop for cute animal and toddler videos, the site is also becoming more accepted as a place to obtain serious news. During the 2011 Arab Spring, for example, YouTube disseminated information by allowing protesters to upload and share videos featuring political commentary. It also launched a single location for live US election coverage in 2012, called the YouTube Elections Hub. It featured content from a wide range of news entities, including ABC News, Al Jazeera English, and BuzzFeed. YouTube recently helped scientists piece together the trajectory and place of impact for a large meteor that fell to Earth in Russia in February 2013. Scientists studied the huge number of videos that Russians had posted of the incoming meteor to perform real science on the behavior of the meteor.

Microblogging Attracts Millions

Twitter, the microblogging platform that uses texting as its forum, also increased the ability of users to stay connected. Launched in 2006, the site has become as wildly popular as Facebook or YouTube. Twitter has more than 200 million users, with about 460,000 new accounts being created each day. More than 140 million tweets are sent each day. As Steven Johnson, author of *The Invention of Air*, puts it, "This is what the naysayers fail to understand: it's just as easy to use Twitter to spread the word about a brilliant 10,000 word *New Yorker* article as it is to spread the word about your Lucky Charms habit."[13]

Entertainers are common users of Twitter, communicating thoughts and locations of underground concerts to their many fans. A vast array of other users, from well-known authors texting about readings to politicians tweeting political musings, have made the site invaluable to their followers. In addition, Twitter

Social Media and the Loss of Privacy

During a demonstration at the British Young Journalist Academy, journalist Joanna Geary showed just how easy it is to track down information about people from seemingly insignificant threads on social media. With one Twitter update picked at random from a search of four key words, Geary was able to identify and locate that Twitter user's entire family in nine steps, which included using Google, LinkedIn, and Facebook.

Geary observed, "It frightens me how simple it was to get all that I did. . . . I've gone from one tweet to knowing an entire family's names, location, address, contact details, what they look like, how they are connected to the military and, potentially, where a part of the US army is coming under fire. I stop there because I am already completely freaked out by just how far I've already got from a few Google searches."

Quoted in Graeme McMillan, "Nine Degrees of Separation: How Easily Your Personal Info Can Be Found Online," *Time*, August 3, 2011. http://techland.time.com.

feeds are responsible for gathering ordinary people to participate in mass events known as "flash mobs." In such events sometimes hundreds of people team up with professionals to learn dances or music and give surprise performances in public places, to the shock and amusement of passersby.

Others have used the site as a simple way to raise money. Private individuals as well as podcasts have used Twitter to get followers to donate money. Ira Glass, host of *This American Life*, for example, regularly asks potential donors to use Twitter to support the popular podcast. And in 2008 Aaron Durand used Twitter to boost sales at his mother's independent bookstore—Broadway Books in Portland, Oregon—which had been hit hard by the worsening US economy. He tweeted about his mom's plight, adding that he would buy a burrito for anyone who bought fifty dollars' worth of books during the holidays at his mom's shop. The Tweet was retweeted again and again. It was so effective that new customers entered the store, and Durand's mother had her best holiday season ever. The store continues to be popular.

Even scientists on the International Space Station who live far above Earth for long periods are able to use Twitter to stay connected to friends, family, and coworkers. The first tweet from space took place in May 2009 when Mike Massimino sent this message: "Launch was awesome!! . . . The adventure of a lifetime has begun!"[14] The National Aeronautics and Space Administration (NASA) has given its support to the use of social networking by space station scientists. In 2010 NASA said that access to social media would help "ease the isolation associated with life in a closed environment."[15]

Smartphones

With the arrival of smartphones, the digital age exploded because people had handheld access to the Internet at all times of the day and night. The mobile phones that made this possible first appeared in the early 2000s. The BlackBerry smartphone became the first to offer wireless e-mail in 2002. When Barack Obama was elected president in 2008, he expressed his fondness for his BlackBerry when he speculated that he would have to give it up for security reasons when he took office: "I'm still clinging to my BlackBerry. . . . They're going to have to pry it out of my hands."[16] Ultimately, Obama was allowed to keep the smartphone.

Using these phones, people could communicate, find information, and conduct business literally anytime and anywhere outside of the physical structures of schools, businesses, and offices. New articles talked of people's addiction to their smartphones—having the urge to continually check the phones for e-mail messages or Facebook posts even when at dinner or socializing with others. Larry D. Rosen, author of *iDisorder: Understanding Our Obsession with Technology and Overcoming Its Hold on Us*, writes about people's attachment to their phones, which he says "have gone from extravagant devices to appendages." He continues:

As smartphones replace flip cell phones these devices will become even more a part of our 24/7 world. According to a 2011 study of more than 3,500 people from 1,100 large corporations worldwide, 61 percent of those surveyed keep their cell phone in the bedroom and more than four in ten have it within arm's reach while they sleep. If you just look at the . . . [younger] employees, those figures shoot up to 77 percent and 60 percent, respectively. Those who keep their phone close to the bed are 60 percent more likely than average to wake during the night to check their phones.[17]

The Internet and the Global Financial Crisis

According to William Davidow, author of *Overconnected: The Promise and Threat of the Internet*, widespread Internet connectivity helped fuel the 2008 financial crisis that was marked by the collapse of large financial institutions, governmental bailouts of banks, and plunging housing and stock markets:

> The Internet did not cause the global economic crisis; cheap money, lax regulation, and unchecked avarice did. What the Internet did was act as an accelerant, spreading information very quickly. It was gasoline on the flames. A crisis of this dimension would not have been possible without a very efficient, fast, cheap, and reliable information transportation system. Across the worldwide digital sprawl, things go viral at lightning speed. And people were carried away in a competitive, greedy fervor of their own creation.

William Davidow, *Overconnected: The Promise and Threat of the Internet*. New York: Delphinium, 2011, p. 8.

Side by side with the development of smartphones was the development of apps, or applications for the phones. These applications range from using the latest GPS technology to upload turn-by-turn directions, to identifying flora and fauna while on a hike, to downloading movies or television shows to watch on one's phone.

The astoundingly rapid development of smartphones and the seemingly infinite variety of applications created for them are eclipsed only by the speed and scope of their acceptance among people of all ages and backgrounds. Davidow describes how all the technological innovations spawned by the Internet have made online activities an inextricable part of modern life:

> What amazes me most about the Internet is the swift and sweeping ways it has affected so many people's lives. We entertain ourselves differently because of the Internet. We shop differently. We get our news differently. We socialize differently. We conduct political campaigns differently. We structure businesses differently. We work differently and we play differently. The railroad, automobile, telephone, radio, and television all affected us but not as deeply and broadly—and not nearly as quickly.[18]

Far-Reaching Impact of All This Connectivity

The Internet and all the devices and services that enable people to use it have led to an unprecedented ability to access information. Clay A. Johnson, author of *The Information Diet: A Case for Conscious Consumption*, says that "the sheer amount of information available to us is mind-boggling." He argues that "today, you're likely to spend upwards of 11 hours per day consuming information—reading books like this, checking out your friends' Facebook pages, reading the newspaper, watching television, listening to the radio or your portable music player. For many of us who work in front of a computer all day, it's even more: we spend all day reading and writing in front of a screen."[19]

Search engines such as Google, moreover, effectively help people access all of this information that is available through the Internet.

As Heather Pringle writes in *Archaeology* magazine, "Google is an astonishing boon to humanity, gathering up and concentrating information and ideas that were once scattered so broadly around the world that hardly anyone could profit from them."[20]

The Internet also allows for an unprecedented ability to collaborate and connect with others. The nature of cyberspace allows ordinary people to collaborate on new ideas or engage in a rapid exchange of information like never before. Using technologies like forums, blogs, and chat rooms, large numbers of people engage in the process of exchanging information. This new type of communication, called crowdsourcing, allows users to provide feedback on a given topic. The application TipJar, for instance, amasses money-saving tips from around the globe. TripAdvisor relies on reviews of millions of members for people looking for a flight, hotel, or vacation. The online encyclopedia *Wikipedia* is one of the most well-known examples of crowdsourcing. Created exclusively by individuals adding its content, the source is now used, sometimes exclusively, by people who want a quick overview of a topic. According to *Wikipedia*'s website, "We want you to imagine a world in which every single human being can freely share in the sum of all knowledge."[21]

"Google is an astonishing boon to humanity, gathering up and concentrating information and ideas that were once scattered so broadly around the world that hardly anyone could profit from them."[20]

— Science writer Heather Pringle.

Businesses also use crowdsourcing to their advantage. Companies use social networking sites, including their own presence on Facebook, to encourage fans to recommend new products. The Ben and Jerry's ice cream company, for example, ran a campaign in 2010 called Do the World a Flavor, in which users on its site could recommend the next ice cream flavor. In 2012 potato chip company Lay's asked its Facebook fans to name its next potato chip flavor, offering a $1 million prize to the winner.

One unusual example of this type of crowdsourcing is a company named uBiome. The company is attempting to use online crowdsourcing to map the human microbiome, the complex ecosystems of bacteria living on and in the human body. "Think of yourself as a place where bacteria lives," said uBiome cofounder

The arrival of smartphones, such as this Apple iPhone, made possible around-the-clock handheld access to the Internet. Smartphones have made it possible to communicate, find information, and conduct business in any setting.

Jessica Richman. "By measuring what's there, we can learn what is going on in our bodies."[22] Biophysicists and biologists at uBiome are appealing directly to people via the web. The company will use samples from around the world to build a catalog of bacteria, viruses, and microorganisms. Participants use a do-it-yourself kit to swab the ear, nose, mouth, belly button, and genital area. The results are shipped back to uBiome, which will post data and graphs online. The company hopes to be the first to engage citizen scientists in 196 countries to help in its project.

Risks and Benefits

One risk of this burst of online communication, however, is a loss of privacy. Unprecedented amounts of personal information are available online, and much of that information is easily accessible to anyone who cares to track it down. Employers and prospective colleges, for example, are increasingly looking at Facebook pages and other online social media to gather information on job and college applicants. A survey of medical school and residency admissions officers found that while only 9 percent mined Facebook for information on applicants, 52 percent would consider evidence of unprofessional behavior on the site as counting against the applicant.

And while the Internet is often touted as a boon to teens and to people who share any number of interests, it can also be a place where those of extreme, destructive beliefs connect. Whereas political extremists may have found it difficult to connect with one another in the past, for example, the Internet makes such connections easy and potentially catastrophic. As Davidow writes:

> Research has found that the number of hate groups in the United States has grown rapidly since the 9/11 attacks on the World Trade Center. Experts hold that the Internet is the primary factor in this increase. Although hate groups have hitherto used conventional media to communicate with their members and attract new ones, the Internet has provided them with audiences. For example, the likes of white supremacists have historically been isolated in various communities. The Internet has made it easier for them to contact one another, reinforce their beliefs, and add to the power of their movement.[23]

"Over the past few years I've had an uncomfortable sense that someone, or something, has been tinkering with my brain, remapping the neural circuitry, reprogramming the memory."[24]

— Writer Nicholas Carr.

Many hate groups have benefited from online recruitment. One new Nazi group whose slogan is "White Pride Worldwide" used Facebook to look for members and spread its hateful ideology before Facebook banned the group from its site. Others have reached out to potential members through online forums and other online sites.

Yet the Internet also has the power to galvanize people who are seeking political and social change, including efforts to overthrow oppression. On the global stage, citizens armed with smartphones have used Twitter and other online communications to demand changes in authoritarian governments. Starting in 2009, for example, Iranians used Twitter to tell thousands of interested people where to meet for antigovernment protests. At the turn of the century, news commentators even started coining terms like *digital democracy*, *virtual democracy*, and *cyberdemocracy* to describe how these rapidly accelerating technologies influence fledgling efforts to adopt democratic principles.

Unprecedented Change

With the world reduced to Twitter feeds, Facebook posts, and information bites on *Wikipedia*, however, many educators and others worry about decreasing attention spans and loss of the ability to concentrate. A 2008 article by author Nicholas Carr for the *Atlantic* posed this question: "Is Google Making Us Stupid?" Carr says, "Over the past few years I've had an uncomfortable sense that someone, or something, has been tinkering with my brain, remapping the neural circuitry, reprogramming the memory."[24] Like Carr, Bruce Friedman, a pathologist at the University of Michigan Medical School, says the Internet is altering the way he thinks: "I now have almost totally lost the ability to read and absorb a longish article on the web or in print."[25]

Philip Davis, a former student at Cornell University and a blogger for the Society for Scholarly Publishing, says that even if the digital age is changing people's mental habits, these changes are not all bad: "The Internet may have made me a less patient reader, but I think that in many ways, it has made me smarter. More connections to documents, artifacts, and people means more external influences on my thinking and thus on my writing."[26] Indeed, while the Internet may be effectively changing the nature of our brains and chemistry, it is also revolutionizing the way people meet and begin relationships. While friends and new acquaintances are continually being made on websites of like-minded individuals, dating websites have allowed people to use algorithms to meet their next beloved. Whether this is good or bad is subject to much debate. Some see online dating, for example, as a way to meet a much wider group of people than in the usual course of one's life. Others see many of these relationships as superficial.

> "It is possible that the Internet could eventually eclipse friends as the most influential way Americans meet their romantic partners."[27]
>
> — Stanford psychologist Michael J. Rosenfeld.

According to Stanford sociologist Michael J. Rosenfeld:

"History shows us that perhaps a century from now saying, 'I'm not an Internet person' may be much like saying 'I don't know how to read.'"[28]

— Writer Clay A. Johnson.

The Internet is the one social arena that is unambiguously gaining in importance over time as a place heterosexual couples meet. For couples who met in 1990 and before, the percentage who met online was essentially zero. Between 1995 and 2005, there was exponential growth in the proportion of respondents who met their partners online, reaching what appears to be a plateau at approximately 22%. For heterosexual couples who met in 2009, the Internet was the third most likely way of meeting, after the intermediation of friends, and approximately tied with the bars, restaurants and other public places. With the rise of the Internet as a way couples meet in the past few years, and the concomitant recent decline in the central role of friends, it is possible that the Internet could eventually eclipse friends as the most influential way Americans meet their romantic partners.[27]

The Future

According to Clay A. Johnson, people spend nearly eleven out of every twenty-four hours plugged into texts, e-mails, tweets, gaming, instant messages, online videos, status updates, downloads, and other online connections. As the technologies advance, expectations rise for even faster, more targeted online networks. The proliferation of the Internet and related technologies is so pervasive that Johnson says, "History shows us that perhaps a century from now saying, 'I'm not an Internet person' may be much like saying 'I don't know how to read.'"[28]

Facts

- There was tremendous growth in social networking in 2009. That year Morgan Stanley reported that time spent on social networking sites increased 82 percent over the previous year.
- According to a 2011 issue of *Consumer Reports*, 1 million children were harassed or threatened via Facebook that year.
- The American Osteopathic Association reported in 2011 that 85 percent of parents of youth aged thirteen to seventeen report that their child has some type of social networking account.
- A report from the National IT User Center in 2010 reports that apparently meaningless or superficial comments and status updates on Facebook actually constitute highly useful networks that allow people to connect with others to receive advice about jobs, housing, and a slew of practical problems.
- A 2010 Stanford University study reported that Internet access at home increases the likelihood that adults will be in a romantic relationship, allegedly because the Internet provides a more efficient way for couples to meet one another.
- According to Nicholas Carr, who has written extensively on the societal impact of the Internet, office workers check their inboxes thirty to forty times an hour.
- A 2011 study at the National University of Singapore found that taking breaks to browse the Internet refreshes tired workers and actually increases productivity in the workplace.

CHAPTER TWO

How Do Online Activities Affect Youth?

In the twenty-first century, young people are exposed to and/or own more technical gadgetry than previously known to humankind. Technology has become so inexpensive and so pervasive that even toddlers are likely to be allowed "screen time"—playing simple games in front of a computer. As Hanna Rosin states in an article in the *Atlantic*, "Without seeming to think much about it or resolve how they felt, parents began giving their devices over to their children to mollify, pacify, or otherwise engage them."[29] According to the Joan Ganz Cooney Center, which studies media and children, by 2010 two-thirds of children aged four to seven had used an iPhone. Older children are likely to have their own cell phones, and most are allowed online activities that include playing games, texting, e-mailing, and using the Internet.

Many parents and educators worry that technology is replacing real experiences and relationships. One stepmother of a preteen boy complained, "He has no friends that actually come to the house. He says he has friends, including a girlfriend, but the only contact they have, except for school, is by texting. He never leaves the house to go to a friend's house for a real experience."[30]

The pervasiveness of online activities is without question. An extensive study at Ball State University in 2009 found that most Americans spend at least eight hours a day looking at a television, computer monitor, or the screen of their mobile phone. For young people these figures are even higher, and these devices are often used simultaneously. As Tony Dokoupil writes in a 2012 article titled "Is the Web Driving Us Mad?":

> In less than a span of a single childhood, Americans have merged with their machines, staring at a screen for at least eight hours a day, more time than we spend on any other activity including sleeping. Teens fit some seven hours of screen time into the average school day; 11, if you count time spent multitasking on several devices. . . .
>
> Meanwhile, texting has become like blinking: the average person, regardless of age, sends or receives about 400 texts a month, four times the 2007 number. The average teen processes an astounding 3,700 texts a month, double the 2007 figure.[31]

Engaged or Distracted Students?

Nor does school offer a break from online activities. In fact, the ideal school is seen as one that allows time handling and learning to use a computer—called "digital literacy" by educators. Some schools that are short on the devices are developing BYOT (bring your own technology) policies—allowing students to use their own cell phones, laptops, and tablets in class so that teachers can use the many online applications to enhance lesson plans. Although students are using many different devices, all can upload the same application. "The Internet is the great equalizer," contends Lenny Schad, an administrator in a school district near Houston. "On a smartphone, there are no limitations. . . . This is the world they live in and we're bringing it into the classroom."[32]

"The Internet is the great equalizer. . . . On a smartphone, there are no limitations. . . . This is the world [students] live in and we're bringing it into the classroom."[32]

— School administrator Lenny Schad.

Many teachers find that the Internet offers educational applications that are fun and interesting and incorporate them into lessons as a way to keep students engaged. Yet the advantages and disadvantages to the use of technology in school are still being investigated.

A study of more than one thousand students in the United Kingdom published in 2012 indicated that students without Internet access were at a disadvantage compared with their wired schoolmates. Researcher Rebecca Eynon commented on the study, "Our qualitative research shows that these disconnected young people are clearly missing out both educationally and socially."[33]

While US studies confirm these findings, according to a Pew Research Center Internet study, technology also distracts students. In focus groups with Advanced Placement and National Writing Project teachers, Pew found that 87 percent believed that today's technologies are leading to a more distracted youth population. Yet 99 percent of teachers agree that the Internet gives students access to a wider range of resources than would otherwise be available to them. These conclusions seem to indicate that while the Internet may allow students to quickly find and incorporate new research into their work, they are less likely to read widely and may get frustrated when they cannot find a result quickly.

Online Learning

Studies such as these are becoming important tools for understanding the effects of technology on education as an increasingly large number of schools strive to make use of new technologies. More than 1 million students in the United States take classes online, and some go through their entire college experience without ever having actually experienced a "live" classroom. Colleges and universities see online education as a boon. They are able to offer a greater number of classes more cheaply, while expanding course offerings and access to classes that are filled. Scott Brady, a geography professor at California State University–Chico, points out that universities are being forced to offer online alternatives: "The [California universities] are being asked to serve more students, and they're getting smaller contributions from the state. So they have to figure something out."[34]

Many educators fear that these trends will not serve students in the long run. They decry the possible loss of the give and take of an actual classroom, with students engaged in dialogue with a teacher and a teacher able to grasp what students are and are not

understanding. This interaction, they say, is an essential part of learning that simply does not exist in online courses. Mark Edmundson, an English professor at the University of Virginia and the author of *Why Read?*, believes that online courses are harming education:

> Online education is a one-size-fits-all endeavor. It tends to be a monologue and not a real dialogue. The Internet teacher, even one who responds to students via e-mail, can never have the immediacy of contact that the teacher on the scene can, with his sensitivity to unspoken moods and enthusiasms. This is particularly true of online courses for which the lectures are already filmed and in the can.[35]

Most schools now have computers or computer labs, but many colleges and universities have gone further, adding online courses to their class offerings. Such courses provide flexibility for working students but also raise concerns about loss of interaction between students and teachers.

No Privacy in a Digital World

People who grow up in today's digital world will have a vast amount of digital data amassed about them, including medical records, tax returns, marriage certificates, traffic violations, and so on. In their book *Born Digital: Understanding the First Generation of Digital Natives*, John Palfrey and Urs Gasser explain that this will have an especially profound impact on young people:

> The digital identity of any citizen of a wired society is composed not only of the data elements that this person contributes voluntarily, but also of the elements that *other* people contribute and collect about him or her. For young people, it's even harder than for those less engaged in digital cultures to control digital identity, given the ubiquity of information about one's friends online. The ramifications for the security and privacy of these individuals are substantial. Those ramifications will only grow over time.

John Palfrey and Urs Gasser, *Born Digital: Understanding the First Generation of Digital Natives*. New York: Basic Books, 2008, p. 41.

Although many students find the 24-7 convenience of online education a boon, especially if they must work to put themselves through college, others feel that they are missing out on the live classroom experience. Student Danielle Andrade says that the courses are convenient, but that "online courses are harder for me personally because I need that face-to-face interaction."[36]

Online education might not satisfy the needs of all students or even all educators, but this form of teaching is very likely here to stay. Those who fear it, says Hanna Rosin, should be mindful of the past. As she says, "Every new medium has, within a short time of its introduction, been condemned as a threat to young people.

Pulp novels would destroy their morals, TV would wreck their eyesight, video games would make them violent."[37]

Brain Changes

Many commentators believe that online technology is having an unprecedented impact on the human brain. Neurologists know that the brain has a certain amount of plasticity, meaning that neural circuitry can be changed and respond to repeated stimuli. Many worry that the Internet may have profound effects on this circuitry. The brain changes, moreover, may be far more pronounced in children and even toddlers, who are now growing up spending countless hours in front of a computer screen. What meaning these brain changes might have for individuals and society is still uncertain.

Nicholas Carr, author of *The Shallows: What the Internet Is Doing to Our Brains*, argues that the neural rewiring wrought by the Internet encourages rapid consumption of small bits of information. Surfing the web, for example, leads users to dart about from one link, text, or image to another while being distracted by an onslaught of messages and feeds. Carr argues that this makes users more adept at scanning but impedes the ability to think deeply.

Many researchers share Carr's concerns about the possibility of online technology affecting the ability of the brain to concentrate for lengthy periods. This characteristic is required for reading a long, complex article or piece of fiction. Multiple studies have shown that when people are asked to read text in a linear fashion—with no embedded links—they are able to retain much more of the information than if they are allowed to read the text in a digital format that allows them to click on hyperlinks to advance the text.

Positive Changes?

Some researchers argue that these brain changes are not necessarily negative, just different. They even make the case that the type of long-term memory that once drove the brain may simply be outdated with the advent of digital technology. If one is able to look up facts and other information almost instantaneously, the need to store these facts in the brain may be less important. Science writer Jonah Lehrer uses an analogy to illustrate how Internet use affects thinking. The brain that is affected by the Internet, he says, is similar to a person walking down a busy city street, as opposed to walking in a quiet park. Lehrer says that there is value in both experiences. "The internet is just like a city. It's a trade-off, but in the end we're willing to make the trade-off because it allows all sorts of new connections."[38]

That the Internet allows the human brain to forget so much may actually be helpful, because it means more capacity for other information. Lehrer argues:

> Just as we learn through . . . memory who knows what in our families and offices, we are learning what the computer "knows" and when we should attend to where we have stored information in our computer-based memories. We are becoming symbiotic with our computer tools, growing into interconnected systems that remember less by knowing information than by knowing where the information can be found.[39]

"We are becoming symbiotic with our computer tools, growing into interconnected systems that remember less by knowing information than by knowing where the information can be found."[39]

— Science writer Jonah Lehrer.

Health and science writer Maia Szalavitz argues that many of the conclusions regarding the negative consequences of frequent Internet use are overblown. Just because the technology is rewiring the brain does not mean this is something to fear. Szalavitz writes: "The reality is that any enjoyable activity leads to changes in the brain's pleasure regions if a person engages in it frequently enough. Indeed, any activity we perform repeatedly will lead to brain changes: that's known as learning. Riding a bicycle and playing the violin also rewire the brain, but we don't choose to refer to these changes as 'damage.'"[40]

A body of recent research that focuses on video games appears to back up the assertion that the biological effects brought about by Internet activities are not necessarily negative. Studies have shown, for example, that playing these fast-paced video games appears to improve vision, attention, and spatial skills. With so many young people spending many hours each day playing video games, more research is needed to probe the depth and impact of these neurological changes.

Impact on Interpersonal Skills and Relationships

The Internet and other technologies are not only transforming the human brain but also how people communicate with each other. E-mails, texting, e-chat, social networking, and other forms of online communication have, in many instances, taken the place of face-to-face contact. Many worry that this constant online activity is permanently altering the nature of human interactions, especially with young people, who were the earliest adopters of and biggest consumers of social media.

Researchers led by Larry D. Rosen conclude that when the main form of contact and relationships with others becomes the Internet, people are more likely to demonstrate psychological disorders such as narcissism, which is marked by complete self-absorption, delusions of grandeur, self-love, and other signs. Rosen writes: "The bottom line is that any technology that allows us to function behind a screen—where people cannot see us and we cannot see them or their reactions to our behaviors—presents numerous opportunities to emulate the characteristics in each of the . . . narcissistic signs."[41]

Such self-absorption is evident when individuals need the constant feedback from texts, on Facebook, and in e-mails to maintain their self-esteem. In one study, one young woman who was asked to stay off the Internet for a few days said, "I feel anxious because I don't know if I'm missing something important. I keep thinking I can't wait for this to end because I need to check my e-mail. How many Facebook notifications am I going to have after this?"[42] The woman was not deterred from meeting people face-to-face, but she felt great anxiety at the idea of being separated from her online existence.

Frequent use of online communication, especially when it replaces person-to-person interaction, can lead to feelings of anonymity. Because of this, a person can dissociate themselves from people's real-life reactions, opinions, and personalities. This may lead to

Many studies have raised concerns about the effects of video gaming, especially on the mental health of young people. But recent research suggests that video games might actually improve vision, attention, and spatial skills.

saying and doing things that another person is offended by and also never learning to interact properly. As Rosen observes, "When you are sitting behind a screen, whether it is a computer screen, a tablet screen, or even a small smartphone screen, you cannot see the person at the other end. You may actually feel somewhat anonymous even though the person at the other end might be a good friend."[43]

Developing Meaningful Friendships

In addition to the problem of anonymity, some researchers observe that the ability to amass huge numbers of friends on social networking sites is yet another factor that may be weakening social relationships. Others contend that these friendship networks are no different from relationships of the past. In the early 1990s a British anthropologist named Robin Dunbar studied human group behavior at the Evolutionary Psychology and Behavioural Ecology Research Group at Liverpool University. Dunbar found that the average human being has a friendship circle of approximately 150 individuals and a more intimate clique of 12 people. Dunbar's number of 150 has been used to study social networking communities and assess how online socializing affects real-life relationships.

Much of the research has confirmed that even though the number of friends people have on social networking sites can be massive, the number of close friends is about the same as in the real world. Such studies console people who argue that social networking is making friendship unnecessary or significantly different. Researchers Nicholas Christakis and James Fowler argue that "on Facebook you've got a few close friends and lots of people you barely know. Because the cost of information transmission is so low we end up staying in touch with more acquaintances. But that doesn't mean we have more friends."[44]

In fact, the latest studies seem to point to online communications as less threatening to interpersonal relationships than previously thought. In the article "Coming of Age on the Internet," the authors point out that when teenagers in the mid-1990s seemed to forgo personal relationships for the Internet, experts warned of problems ahead. This view is now changing as social scientists are coming to believe that the psychological benefits of such connections might actually outweigh any detrimental effects. Teens themselves have had an impact on the Internet and have remade it into a true social networking tool. Today more than eight in ten teenagers use instant messaging mediums to connect with the same friends they see at school and work. A study of eight hundred students in South Africa found that those students who were heavily engaged in Facebook reported feelings of psychological well-being, suggesting that online communications benefited students' self-esteem and feelings of self-worth.

In fact, some researchers have found that online contact simply has very little effect on the things teens think about. Researchers Alice Marwick and danah boyd found that "while it's true that teens incorporate social media into many facets of their lives . . . the core elements of high-school life are fundamentally the same today as they were two decades ago: friends, relationships, grades, family, and the future."[45]

Technology's Impact on the Psyche

While almost everyone would agree that the Internet is having an impact on relationships, a consensus is building that technology may be leading to increased anxiety for young people. Today's teens rarely take the time to enjoy the outdoors, read a printed book or newspaper, or simply hang out with friends outside of school. Even at meals in restaurants, the teens at the table are often glancing at e-mail, looking up facts on the Internet, or interrupting the meal to post where they are on Facebook. Many researchers are finding that this translates to a restless mind that can never completely focus on the task at hand. As Tony Dokoupil writes in *Newsweek*:

> The proof is starting to pile up. The first good, peer-reviewed research is emerging, and the picture is much gloomier than the trumpet blasts of Web utopians have allowed. The current incarnation of the Internet—portable, social, accelerated, and all-pervasive—may be making us not just dumber or lonelier but more depressed and anxious, prone to obsessive-compulsive and attention-deficit disorders, even outright psychotic. . . .
>
> Web use often displaces sleep, exercise, and face-to-face exchanges, all of which can upset even the chirpiest soul. But the digital impact may last not only for a day or a week, but for years down the line. A recent American study based on data from adolescent Web use in the 1990s found a connection between time online and mood disorders in young adulthood. Chinese researchers have similarly found "a direct effect" between heavy Net use and the development of full-blown depression, while scholars at Case Western Reserve University correlated heavy texting and social-media use with stress, depression, and suicidal thinking.[46]

"Web use often displaces sleep, exercise, and face-to-face exchanges, all of which can upset even the chirpiest soul."[46]

— Writer Tony Dokoupil.

Educators worry that such mood changes may be especially keen for young people, whose entire social network may be occurring online. Teens who spend an exorbitant amount of time online may be in danger of developing mental health issues such as ag-

"You Can Create Who You Want to Be"

Audrey, a teenager heavily involved in social media, speaks about writing her own social networking profile and why she calls this creating "a performance of you":

> You're creating your own little ideal person and sending it out. . . . You're not going to post pictures of how you look every day. You're going to get your makeup on, put on your cute outfit, you're going to take your picture and post it up as your default, and that's what people are going to expect that you are every day, when really you're making it up for all these people. . . . You can write anything about yourself; these people don't know. You can create who you want to be.

Quoted in Sherry Turkle, *Alone Together: Why We Expect More from Technology and Less from Each Other*. New York: Basic Books, 2011, p. 191.

gression and depression. According to a 2010 study in *Archives of Pediatrics & Adolescent Medicine*, the risk for depression for teens who used the Internet excessively was two and a half times that of their peers. The authors concluded, "Young people who are initially free of mental health problems but use the Internet pathologically could develop depression as a consequence."[47]

Managing an online identity, including reading and responding to constant online feedback, can lead to anxiety and depression. This is especially true for impressionable teens who are still forming their identities. As Dokoupil writes, "[In 2011] when MTV polled its 13- to 30-year-old viewers on their Web habits, most felt 'defined' by what they put online, 'exhausted' by always having to be putting it out there, and utterly unable to look away for fear of missing out."[48]

While much of the news about depression and anxiety comes

from teens who feel driven to use technology constantly, some studies have found that moderate use can help young people. A study of college students found that spending time on Facebook increased relaxation, slowed heart rate, and decreased stress levels. Some young people report that using Facebook improved their feelings about their lives. A study conducted by Keith Campbell at the University of Georgia found that "editing yourself and constructing yourself on these social networking sites, even for a short period of time, seems to have an effect on how you see yourself."[49]

Controlling Technology

Technology will continue to have an enormous impact on teens' everyday interactions—in school, at work, and during free time. For many teens, life itself seems more fast-paced, with less time for reflection than ever. Some commentators believe that technology is not to blame for the many changes it has brought about. It is up to teens, especially as they become adults, to determine what these changes mean and to respond accordingly. Believing that technology is acting upon us rather than the other way around will increase fears and anxiety. Samuel Arbesman, author of *The Half-Life of Facts: Why Everything We Know Has an Expiration Date*, uses Google as an example. He argues that Google is not making teenagers and others who use the Internet obsessively unable to memorize. However, Arbesman points out, learning to use search engines well, including how to ask the right questions so that users get good results, is learning to use a new tool appropriately.

> "Editing yourself and constructing yourself on these social networking sites, even for a short period of time, seems to have an effect on how you see yourself."[49]
>
> — Keith Campbell, a researcher at the University of Georgia.

Every new invention throughout history has given rise to concerns about the potential for bringing about disorder and even ruin. But ultimately, Arbesman and others point out, it is how we use the tools, especially for young people who have never been without them, that will make the difference between success or failure.

Facts

- The Council on Communications and Media reported in 2011 that 25 percent of teen cell phone owners used them to access social media.
- According to the Pew Internet & American Life Project, in 2010, 88 percent of teen cell phone owners used the device to text, 83 percent to take pictures, 54 percent to record videos, and 27 percent for general Internet use. A full 32 percent reported texting while driving.
- A 2010 Kaiser Family Foundation study reported that teens spend roughly one and a half hours a day texting, averaging approximately 118 text messages a day.
- Research from the University of California–San Diego and the University of Scranton in Pennsylvania in 2012 reported that among students, Facebook posts were about one and a half times more memorable than sentences of written text and two and a half times more memorable than pictures of faces.
- According to 2009 research at Stanford University, those who reported heavy media multitasking scored lower on cognitive tests than those who reported only light multitasking.

CHAPTER THREE

Are Online Activities Addictive?

The topic of addiction has become controversial. News stories abound about whether certain activities can become a true addiction. Most of the controversy lies in whether a person's urge to participate is a documented physical dependence, such as addiction to drugs and alcohol, or an undocumented addiction, such as eating compulsively. Many claim that activities such as eating too much junk food, shopping until one goes into debt, and other "addictions" may be just bad behavior. Yet as scientists discover more about the brain, they are redefining what constitutes addiction.

Since more people seem to have an uncontrollable urge to use devices such as smartphones for checking e-mail, computers to post updates and play online games, and a host of other activities, scientists have been looking into whether it is possible to become addicted to such activities. According to a Stanford University School of Medicine study, one out of eight Americans suffers from Internet addiction. It also appears to be a global problem: Studies in other countries, including Italy, Pakistan, Korea, and Taiwan, have documented Internet addiction, and China in particular views the affliction as a serious public health problem. In fact, China may become the first nation to make this addiction a medical disorder. China's medical professionals define an Internet addict as anyone who spends at least 6.13 hours online each day.

Despite such changes in attitude, medical professionals find that defining such behaviors as addictive remains problematic.

Dave Mosher, who wrote a 2011 *Scientific American* article on Internet addiction, discusses the problem of redefining addiction for the medical profession:

> Loosely defined, addiction is a disease of the brain that compels someone to obsess over, obtain and abuse something, despite unpleasant health or social effects. And "internet addiction" definitions run the gamut, but most researchers similarly describe it as excessive (even obsessive) Internet use that interferes with the rhythm of daily life.
>
> Yet unlike addictions to substances such as narcotics or nicotine, behavioral addictions to the Internet, food, shopping and even sex are touchy among medical and brain researchers. Only gambling seems destined to make it into

A young man undergoes electrotherapy at a Beijing, China, center for people addicted to online games and other online activities. China considers Internet addiction to be a serious public health problem.

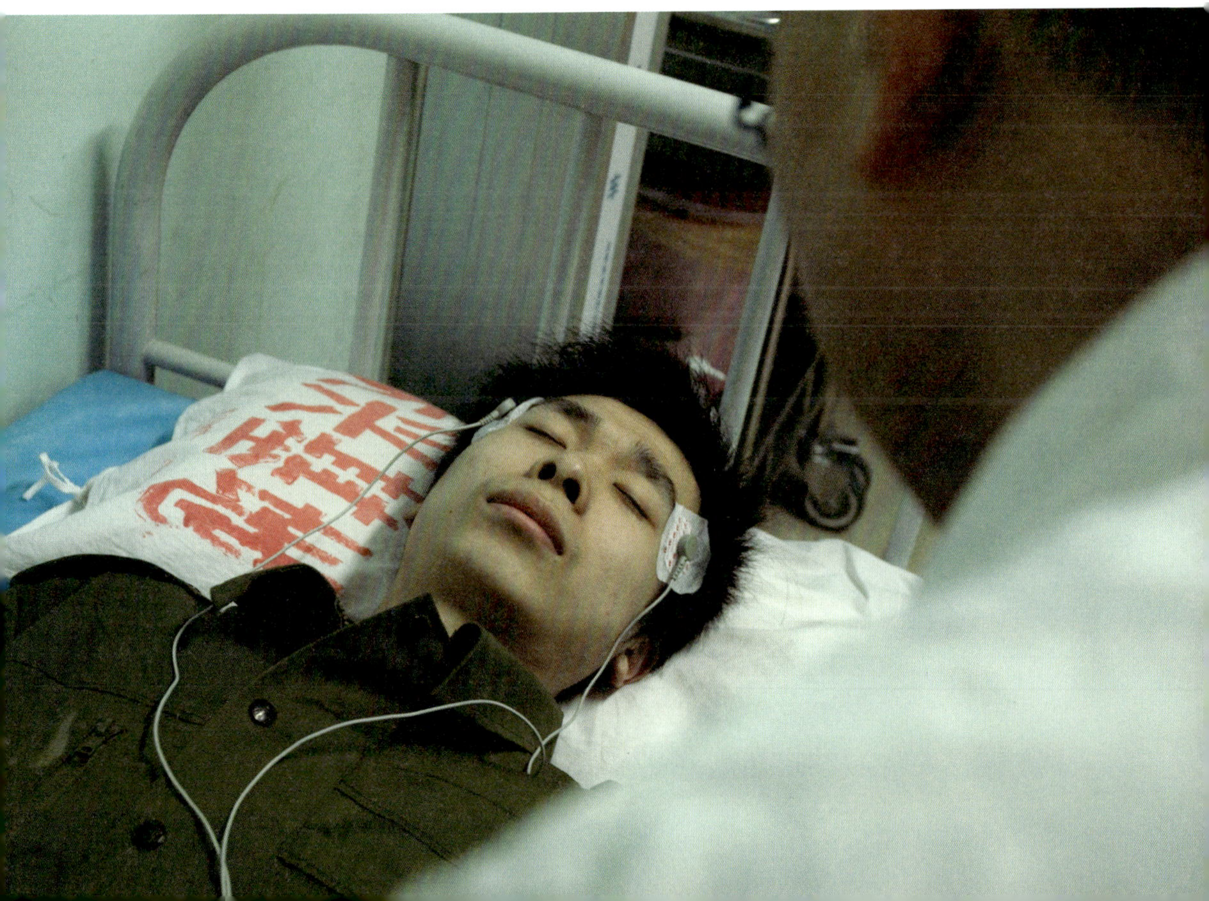

the next iteration of the *Diagnostic and Statistical Manual of Mental Disorders*, or DSM, the internationally recognized bible of things that can go awry with the brain.[50]

Reward System in the Brain

Much of the research into Internet addiction centers on the brain, specifically the reward centers of the brain. This research was first pioneered by psychologist B.F. Skinner more than fifty years ago. Skinner's experiments with rats and pigeons proved that when these animals were rewarded with some regularity for performing a certain activity, their brains consistently released dopamine, a neurotransmitter that regulates pleasure. Researchers believe that, just like Skinner's animals, people's Internet habits may be rewarding them with a shot of dopamine. In essence, whenever someone receives a text, tweet, or other social media feedback, the compulsion to check it may be backed up by a dopamine surge.

> "Dopamine makes us seek, which causes us to receive more dopamine, which causes us to seek more. That jolt you feel when you get a new email in your inbox, or hear the sound of your cell phone's ding? That's dopamine and it puts you in a frenzy."[52]
>
> — Writer Clay A. Johnson.

As Hilarie Cash, executive director of a rehabilitation program for Internet addiction, says, "Internet addiction is the same as any other addiction—excessive release of dopamine. . . . Addiction is addiction. Whether it's gambling, cocaine, alcohol, or Facebook."[51]

Research into dopamine, then, is essential to studying the Internet's impact on human behavior. According to writer and commentator Clay A. Johnson:

> Dopamine makes us seek, which causes us to receive more dopamine, which causes us to seek more. That jolt you feel when you get a new email in your inbox, or hear the sound of your cell phone's ding? That's dopamine and it puts you in a frenzy. This used to be helpful: our dopamine systems helped us, as a species, to find resources, acquire knowledge, and innovate. But in an age of abundance, there are new consequences.
>
> Dopamine receptors often put us in a loop. With all the inputs available to us today—all the various places where notifications come about: our email boxes, our text mes-

A "First World Problem"

Science and technology writer Clay A. Johnson believes that people must learn to manage how they consume the abundant information available in a hyperconnected world:

> It's the best "first world problem" there is. "Oh, my inbox is so full," or, "I just can't keep up with all the tweets and status updates and emails" are common utterances of the digital elite. Though we constantly complain of it—of all the news, and emails, and status updates, and tweets, and the television shows that we feel compelled to watch—the truth is that information is not requiring you to consume it. It can't: information is no more autonomous than fried chicken, and it has no ability to force you to do anything as long as you are aware of how it affects you. There has always been more human knowledge and experience than any one human could absorb. It's not the total amount of information, but your information habit that is pushing you to whatever extreme you find uncomfortable.

Clay A. Johnson, *The Information Diet: A Case for Conscious Consumption*. Sebastopol, CA: O'Reilly, 2012, p. 25.

sages, our various social network feeds, and blogs to read—our brains throw us into a runaway loop in which we're not able to focus on a given task at hand. Rather, we keep pursuing new dopamine reinforcement from the deluge of notifications headed our way.[52]

Not only are brain chemicals involved when a person obsessively uses the Internet, the brain's actual circuitry may change to incorporate the experience. The brain can form new neural circuitry that compels people to repeat an activity to get the same "high." While the brain is flexible and can adapt readily to new experiences, the new neural pathways cry out to be activated again and again. One of the unwelcome effects of this adaptation is that it can lock people into rigid habits, like obsessively checking e-mail, tweets, and Facebook posts.

Author Nicholas Carr writes of his own brain's adaptations this way:

> It wasn't just that so many of my habits and routines were changing as I became more accustomed to and dependent on the sites and services of the Net. The very way my brain worked seemed to be changing. It was then that I began worrying about my inability to pay attention to one thing for more than a couple of minutes. At first I'd figured that the problem was a symptom of middle-age mind rot. But my brain, I realized, wasn't just drifting. It was hungry. It was demanding to be fed the way the Net fed it—and the more it was fed, the hungrier it became. Even when I was away from my computer, I yearned to check e-mail, click links, do some Googling. I wanted to be *connected*.[53]

"The current explosion of digital technology not only is changing the way we live and communicate but is rapidly and profoundly altering our brains."[54]

— Gary Small, head of the Memory and Aging Research Center at the University of California–Los Angeles.

Gary Small, head of the Memory and Aging Research Center at the University of California–Los Angeles, was able to document changes—some of which could lead to Internet addiction—in the brain during moderate Internet use. Small scanned the brains of twenty-four people, half of whom had never used the Internet and half who had. The difference in the scan was striking, especially in the alteration of the prefrontal cortex in the web users. Small then asked the non-web users to spend five hours online and return for another brain scan. "The naïve subjects had already rewired their brains," Small wrote. He concluded that "the current explosion of digital technology not only is changing the way we live and communicate but is rapidly and profoundly altering our brains." Small says that using computers, smartphones, and other technology "stimulates brain cell altera-

The Only Solution for Addiction

Massachusetts Institute of Technology professor Sherry Turkle explains why society should not contemplate excessive Internet use in terms of addiction:

> It is, of course, tempting to talk about [excessive online activity] in terms of addiction. . . . The addiction metaphor fits a common experience: the more time spent online, the more one wants to spend time online. But however apt the metaphor, we can ill afford the luxury of using it. Talking about addiction subverts our best thinking because it suggests that if there are problems, there is only one solution. To combat addiction, you have to discard the addicting substance. But we are not going to "get rid" of the Internet. We will not go "cold turkey" or forbid cell phones to our children. We are not going to stop the music or go back to television as the family hearth. I believe we will find new paths toward each other, but considering ourselves victims of a bad substance is not a good first step. The idea of addiction, with its one solution that we know we won't take, makes us feel hopeless. We have to find a way to live with seductive technology and make it work for our purposes.

Sherry Turkle, *Alone Together: Why We Expect More from Technology and Less from Each Other*. New York: Basic Books, 2011, pp. 293–94.

tion and neurotransmitter release, gradually strengthening new neural pathways in our brains while weakening old ones."[54] Once these neural pathways in the brain have been reinforced, performing the behaviors associated with them can be hard to resist and can lead to dependence.

Transformed Thinking

The Chinese have also documented the effects of Internet addiction. The Chinese are considered pioneers in the field because they have been studying the phenomenon longer than have other nations. According to a Chinese study published in June 2012 in *PLoS ONE*, Internet addiction does indeed rewire the brain. In fact, when brain scans are performed on so-called Internet addicts (people who spend more than eight hours a day on the Internet), their brains look very similar to those addicted to drugs and alcohol. Chinese researchers noted that they found extra nerve cells built for speed in areas devoted to attention, control, and executive function. The brain had atrophied—shrinking 10 to 20 percent—in areas responsible for processing memory, motor control, speech, emotion, and sensory information. And worse, the more time spent online, the more the brain atrophied.

"In online games you can become a hero, build empires, and submerge yourself in a fantasy. That kind of escapism is what draws young people."[58]

— Neuroscientist Karen M. von Deneen.

These studies show that the Internet is allowing for an entirely different learning and cultural milieu that is transforming the way people think. As journalist Tony Dokoupil writes, "The research is now making it clear that the Internet is not 'just' another delivery system. It is creating a whole new mental environment, a digital state of nature where the human mind becomes a spinning instrument panel, and few people will survive unscathed."[55]

Detractors, however, argue that such research proves little. People seek out anything that is pleasurable to them and seek to continue the activity. Psychologist Peter Gray points out, "If we were to define every activity that activates the brain's 'pleasure centers' as addictive, and therefore to be curtailed, we would have to curtail everything that's fun. . . . We've got neuroscientists saying, 'if it lights up the pleasure centers, beware of it!' Especially if it does so in kids."[56] Whether online activities become an issue, then, seems up to the individual. A person who drinks one or two glasses of wine is not deemed an alcoholic, just as a person who checks their e-mail occasionally may not be deemed an addict.

Online Gaming

One addictive behavior that parents and educators are particularly nervous about is online gaming, because it mostly affects young people, whose brains are still developing. Hilarie Cash says:

> Internet and video game addiction starts young. Most young men are given computer or video games when they are five or six years old and therefore their childhood development is profoundly wired for these activities. It's quite different to drug addicts and alcoholics who are usually exposed to drugs or alcohol closer to the age of 15. Internet addicts usually have 15 to 20 years of addiction on them due to starting younger.[57]

Gaming addiction is not just an American phenomenon; it affects young people worldwide. The Chinese have found their young people especially prone to it. Neuroscientist Karen M. von Deneen explains the appeal: "Americans don't have a lot of personal time, but Chinese seem to have even less. They work 12 hours a day, six days a week. They work very, very hard. Sometimes the Internet is their greatest and only escape. . . . In online games you can become a hero, build empires, and submerge yourself in a fantasy. That kind of escapism is what draws young people."[58]

Indeed, the escapist nature of role-playing games seems especially addictive to young males, who are the majority of users. These games are attractive to boys and men who have poor self-esteem or problems making friends. Games in which the more one plays, the more powerful and influential one's role-playing character becomes seem especially addictive. Some researchers believe that the games are especially designed to keep players online. Others believe that the outlet provides a much-needed boost to such young men, allowing them to find others like them online and to have more control over their world. As Gray states:

> People play games because they are challenging, fun, and conducive to social interaction with other gamers; but they are bombarded by messages from the larger culture suggesting that gaming is a sign of laziness, is "addictive,"

> and leads to all sorts of ill effects, and so they become concerned about gaming. People who spend similar amounts of time at chess, or reading English literature, or skiing, don't get these messages.[59]

Gray believes that because online gaming is new, people have stereotyped gamers, further isolating them. He argues that gaming is like any other activity, and if the activity begins to take over one's life, it is a personal time-management issue, not an addiction.

Other social scientists believe, however, that gaming takes the place of activities that all young people must master. According to Keith Bakker, director of Smith & Jones Addiction Consultants, such activities can affect the normal development of a child, "Children who play four to five hours per day have no time for socializing, doing homework, or playing sports. That takes away from normal social development. You can get a 21-year-old with the emotional intelligence of a 12-year-old. He's never learned to talk to girls. He's never learned to play a sport."[60]

Social Media

Unlike online gaming, which affects mostly young men, the use of Facebook and other social media is more widespread. Ninety-eight percent of the US online population uses some sort of social media. Facebook accounts for 55 percent of those users. The female population spends an average of just under eight hours a month on online social media tools, and males spend about six. Other top sites that are gaining members include Twitter, Tumblr, and Google+. Fueling the growth is the smartphone market. A poll taken in October 2011 showed that 64 percent of US Internet users had accessed social networking sites at least once. Most people—70 to 80 percent—use the phone to check posts or post something themselves. Finally, close to 54 percent use their phones to follow celebrities or follow posts about organizations, brands, or events. According to the American Medical Association, 68.9 percent of Americans are regular Internet users, with

> "Children who play [online games] four to five hours per day have no time for socializing, doing homework, or playing sports. That takes away from normal social development."[60]
>
> — Keith Bakker, director of Smith & Jones Addiction Consultants.

13.7 percent claiming it is difficult to stay away from the Internet for more than a day and 5.9 percent admitting that their relationships suffer because of constant Internet use. Clearly, people use their phones as online networking tools, but is such use becoming obsessive or addictive?

Enthusiasts test new games at a gaming fair in Germany in 2011. Online role-playing games can be especially addictive, although researchers have mixed views on whether this is harmful or not.

In a 2012 poll of 423 students, researchers in Norway identified six signs that indicate a Facebook addiction, using a test called the Bergen Facebook Addiction Scale. They are:

- You spend a lot of time thinking about Facebook or plan use of Facebook.
- You feel an urge to use Facebook more and more.
- You use Facebook to forget about personal problems.
- You have tried to cut down on the use of Facebook without success.
- You become restless or troubled if you are prohibited from using Facebook.

- You use Facebook so much that it has had a negative impact on your job/studies.[61]

People who answered these assessments with the response "very often" were deemed addicted to the site. Among mostly younger users (under age twenty-five), the site has become a go-to spot to post every detail of their lives, check in on others, and follow friends' activities. In his book *The Digital Diet*, Canadian writer Daniel Sieberg writes about when he began to realize he was addicted. While scuba diving in the Bahamas, he encountered a massive tiger shark, only to find himself instinctively reaching for his smartphone to post the experience. Sieberg believes that social media may be "systematically, silently and imperceptibly destroying parts of our lives that we hold dear."[62]

Studies Have Mixed Results

Studies seem to be split on whether the social media frenzy is good or bad for people, however. In one South African study released in *Behaviour & Information Technology* in 2013, eight hundred students at seven universities were asked about Facebook. The study found that intense Facebook users had a higher level of psychological well-being, including high rates of self-esteem. Some commentators suggest that posting on Facebook and commenting on others' posts helps build a sense of connection with others, not unlike being part of a high school clique. According to writer Erin Biba, "Every time you post something on Twitter, Facebook, Tumblr, or Instagram, you're influencing—or trying to influence—how the world views you." She says a person creates "the hilarious, adorable, fascinating, intelligent, so-worth-Friending version of you. Social media [is] about advertising yourself."[63] Such constructions allow people to remake themselves into a better, more popular version of who they are. And, some researchers say, this inevitably lifts the spirits of the creator.

Other studies have found that Facebook can improve the heart rate by allowing users to relax, help people network to find a job, help people find a mate, improve workforce productivity, and improve the chances of staying in school. Facebook has become just one more pastime to help people feel connected to others, these studies suggest.

But, as with many things in the online world, others disagree, and most of that disagreement centers on the effect of Facebook on the young. According to a 2010 study published in the *Archives of Pediatrics & Adolescent Medicine*, 1,041 teens living in China were asked about their online social networking activities. Of those, 6.2 percent were deemed to have a pathological use of the Internet. Among those users, 87 percent had developed depression. The authors concluded that young people who use the Internet obsessively could develop depression, even if they were initially free of mental health problems.

"Every time you post something on Twitter, Facebook, Tumblr, or Instagram, you're influencing—or trying to influence—how the world views you."[63]

— Writer Erin Biba.

In a study of two German universities released in 2013 called "Envy on Facebook: A Hidden Threat to Users' Life Satisfaction?," researchers found that one in three people felt worse after visiting Facebook. Such people felt envy, loneliness, and misery after viewing their friends' posts. "Passive following triggers invidious emotions, with users mainly envying happiness of others, the way others spend their vacation and socialize,"[64] according to the authors.

Facebook may have an even darker, more sinister effect for a small minority already at risk of mental illness. In a 2012 study at Tel Aviv University, researcher Uri Nitzan found that three of his mental health patients experienced psychotic episodes as a result of spending time on Facebook. Nitzan found that these three patients sought out interaction and friendships on Facebook to create a sort of virtual life. "All of the patients developed psychotic symptoms related to the situation, including delusions regarding the person behind the screen and their connection through the computer."[65] He argues that mental health professionals should be actively asking patients about their Internet use and how much time they spend on Facebook. In a small percentage of the population, Nitzan argues, such patients may be in deep psychological danger. "How people conduct themselves on the Internet is quite important to psychiatrists, who shouldn't ignore this dimension of their patients' behavior patterns."[66]

Further Addictions Haunt Internet Users

While gaming and social media are being studied because they are especially influential in the lives of young people, other online obsessions are being examined, too. Some psychologists have deemed pathological watching of online pornography an addiction, as well as use of sites that encourage online gambling and online shopping. These online addictions have destroyed marriages and endangered people's livelihoods. Online gamblers and shoppers have been known to put their families in hundreds of thousands of dollars in debt as they continue to use credit cards to obsessively play and purchase.

Whether online activities are truly developing into new addictions or whether, as in the past, a small percentage of people will become obsessed about any new fad will be left to future studies. The Internet and smartphone technology are too new to yet determine long-term patterns.

Facts

- **A 2010 joint study by the University of Notre Dame in Australia and the SunYat-Sen University in Guangzhou, China, reported that participants who reported being addicted to the Internet were 2.5 times more likely to be depressed than those who did not report pathological Internet use.**

- **According to the Chinese government, about 10 percent of the country's more than 30 million gamers are addicted to the activity.**

- **A study out of Swansea and Milan Universities published in 2013 reported that Internet addicts suffer withdrawal symptoms similar to those of drug users.**

- **According to multiple studies, eighteen- to twenty-four-year-olds are most likely to exhibit symptoms of Internet addiction.**

CHAPTER FOUR

Do Online Activities Promote Antisocial Behavior?

On September 22, 2010, Tyler Clementi, an eighteen-year-old student at Rutgers University in Piscataway, New Jersey, jumped to his death from the George Washington Bridge. Clementi's suicide was precipitated by the actions of his dormitory roommate, Dharun Ravi, and a fellow hall mate, Molly Wei. Ravi and Wei secretly set up a webcam in the dorm room and watched Clementi kissing another man. The two then wrote about the encounter on a live Twitter feed. This effectively outed the shy Clementi, who committed suicide rather than face the school, his family, and friends. Ravi and Wei's act led to criminal prosecution for a hate crime. The incident also prompted speculation about how cyberspace has made cruelty so much easier and, simultaneously, so much more devastating. In a March 2012 interview with the *New Jersey Star-Ledger*, Ravi answered a question about what he was thinking when he urged friends to check out the webcam images, "I wasn't. . . . I got caught up in what I thought was funny, and my own ego,"[67] This cavalier response seemed to make such cyberacts even more thoughtless. Clearly, the Internet allowed Ravi such distance from his victim that he had no real idea how devastating his actions might be.

The Disinhibition Effect

In the cyberworld, people can re-create themselves. It is not unusual for people to create several online Facebook personas, for example, or create several versions of themselves on online dating profiles to attract various admirers. These alternate personalities are possible because many people bank on either never meeting the other person or, if they do meet, role-playing their online persona. Many times, the online persona is very different from the real-life person—much bolder and more confident. Researchers have named this phenomenon the disinhibition effect. It describes the effect of people undergoing a dramatic loosening of inhibitions while online and helps explain why people can be incredibly mean-spirited or even vicious online, even if they would never display these personality traits in real life.

The disinhibition effect was described by Internet psychologist John Suler in a 2004 article in the journal *CyberPsychology and Behavior*. Suler identified several characteristics that interact with one another to radically alter a user's online personas. Online anonymity, for example, allows people a feeling of safety that might not be present in real-world interactions. As Suler writes, "When people have the opportunity to separate their actions from their real world and identity, they feel less vulnerable about opening up. Whatever they say or do can't be directly linked to the rest of their lives."[68]

"When people have the opportunity to separate their actions from their real world and identity, they feel less vulnerable about opening up. Whatever they say or do can't be directly linked to the rest of their lives."[68]

— Internet psychologist John Suler.

In online environments people typically cannot hear or see the person on the other end of the conversation. Even if the people know each other, not seeing facial expressions and other body language amplifies the disinhibition effect. As Suler explains, "Seeing a frown, a shaking head, a sigh, a bored expression, and many other subtle and not so subtle signs

of disapproval or indifference can slam the brakes on what people are willing to express."[69]

Similarly, because online communication does not require people to interact with one another in real time, users do not have to deal with immediate reactions. As Suler explains, "Immediate, real-time feedback from others tends to have a very powerful effect on the ongoing flow of how much people reveal about themselves."[70] The absence of such feedback contributes to the disinhibiting effect.

Additionally, many people disassociate online fiction from offline fact. They may come to believe that the imaginary characters they have created, in tandem with their own online persona, exist in a make-believe dimension that is separate from the realities and responsibilities of the real world. Suler describes the phenomenon:

> Emily Finch, an author and criminal lawyer studying identity theft in cyberspace, has suggested that some people see

The Internet might encourage cruel acts by putting distance between the victims and perpetrators of online harassment and bullying. One such act involved Dharun Ravi (center, entering courtroom in 2012), who was convicted of bias intimidation involving his roommate, Tyler Clementi.

their online life as a kind of game with rules and norms that don't apply to everyday living. . . . Once they turn off the computer and return to their daily routine, they believe they can leave that game and their game-identity behind. Why should they be held responsible for what happens in that make-believe play world that has nothing to do with reality?[71]

Though the characteristics described by Suler play out in some of the most heinous acts of bullying, disinhibition has also contributed to acts of kindness. Called benign disinhibition, this phenomenon manifests itself when a timid person opens up and shares personal things about him- or herself that help the person connect with others in a positive way. Benign disinhibition allows these people to be less guarded about expressing positive emotions, to become more affectionate and warm toward others, and to express their true self. Socially isolated people may feel less isolated and gain greater confidence.

Benign disinhibition can also propel people's generous side. In online support groups for addicts or people with diseases, for example, people may spend hours helping another person who posts to the site with information, contacts, and words of encouragement. On sites such as Watsi and Kiva, people are able to donate money to individuals all over the world, including lending money to a restaurant owner in the Philippines or helping a nine-year-old girl in Myanmar who needs eye surgery. Such sites allow people to connect to other individuals, spur their empathy for others, and express it, all using the anonymity of the Internet.

Cyberbully Tormenters

Of course, disinhibition is most widely recognized for its devastating consequences, especially in its role in cyberbullying. The online organization OvercomeBullying.org states that in this hyperconnected digital age, bullies have a new weapon with which to torment:

Social isolation, public humiliation and malicious gossip have long been the stock in trade of bullies. With the advent of modern communications such as email, chat, text

Reasons for Cyberbullying

According to the website Internet Safety 101, cyberbullies report many reasons for engaging in the behavior:

- Eleven percent said it was to show off to friends.
- Fourteen percent said it was to be mean.
- Sixteen percent cited a reason not listed in the survey.
- Twenty-one percent said it was to embarrass their victim.
- Twenty-eight percent said it was for fun or entertainment.
- Fifty-eight percent said it was because the victim deserved it.
- Fifty-eight percent said it was to get back at someone.

> messaging and cell phones as well as the ability to publish online on websites, blogs and social networking sites such as Facebook and MySpace making their message instantly available to millions, the bully's reach and powers of social manipulation have been increased exponentially.[72]

In a few well-publicized cases, the cyberbully created such torment for his or her victim that the person committed suicide. That is what happened to Megan Taylor Meier, thirteen, who committed suicide in 2006 after being bullied on MySpace. In that case the mother of an ex-friend of Meier, Lori Drew, created a MySpace page for a fictitious boy named Josh, who became friends with Megan on the site. Josh abruptly stopped being friends with Megan, saying in an online chat, "Everybody in O'Fallon [Megan's town] knows who you are. You are a bad person and everybody hates you. Have a shitty rest of your life. The world would be a better place without you."[73] Megan hanged herself the same day. An investigation by Meier's parents revealed Drew's role. The incident prompted outrage that an adult could go to such lengths to bully a young girl. It also reinforced the anonymity and power of the Internet.

OvercomeBullying.org acknowledges the disinhibition effect at work in these cases: "How can cyber bullies be so heartless? Perhaps the internet lends itself to this indifference. Bullies don't have to see their victims or answer for their actions. Like the cowards they are they hide behind their computers—behind a veil of anonymity."[74]

Reliable statistics regarding cyberbullying are difficult to find, because they vary depending on the age group studied, how it is defined, and how it is quantified. According to 2011 data from the

Experts say that the anonymity of online communication, and the vast reach of messages and videos posted online, eliminate inhibitions and add a sense of boldness to those who engage in cyberbullying. Teens, in particular, say that online bullying is common.

Pew Research Center's Internet & American Life Project, 33 percent of American teens have been victims of cyberbullying. According to the Harris Interactive newsletter *Trends & Tudes*, among thirteen- to seventeen-year-olds this number is even higher, with a full 43 percent in this age group reporting having been cyberbullied. Unfortunately, just as in real-life bullying, others seem to do nothing or join in the torment. According to Pew Research data, 66 percent of teens who have witnessed online cruelty have also witnessed others joining in, and 21 percent admit to joining in themselves.

Anguish and Abuse

There definitely seems to be more fodder for bullying as more immature teens use the Internet without understanding the consequences. Ottawa, Canada, teenager Amanda Todd, fifteen, committed suicide after posting a video about how awful her life had become after she exposed her breasts to an unknown man online, only to have that man post the photo to all her family and friends. Even after Todd moved to another school, the man found her again and posted the photo. Todd continued to be tormented about the picture and became a victim of other bullying stunts at her school. Todd's video portrays not only her anguish, but her insistence that she could never escape the mistake she made in seventh grade. She never learned the name or identity of her bully.

As Kelly McParland writes in Toronto's *National Post*:

> Bullies are notorious cowards. . . . The internet allows the cowards to mask their identity, to strike from the safety of anonymity. Anyone more than marginally familiar with the internet knows there is a very ugly side to the online community; a mob mentality that takes a certain joy in the hounding and tormenting of others. We're talking about people so crude that a memorial page set up for Todd has been plagued by abusive photos and comments, including a photo of a young woman hanging herself with a rope and another of a bottle of bleach and the caption "it's to die for" [Todd had tried to kill herself by drinking bleach at one point].[75]

Another Side of Facebook

A study by Christopher J. Carpenter titled "Narcissism on Facebook: Self-Promotional and Anti-Social Behavior," published in 2012, attempts to explain Facebook's more harmful aspects, such as narcissism. Carpenter defines narcissism as a "pervasive pattern of grandiosity, need for admiration and an exaggerated sense of self importance." The study measured self-promoting Facebook behaviors, such as frequently updating profile information or posting status updates and photos. It also measured several antisocial behaviors, such as seeking retaliation against negative comments and getting angry when others do not comment on status updates. The results showed that scoring higher on the narcissistic personality scale meant a person was more likely to brag and display antisocial behaviors.

Quoted in Western Illinois University, "Facebook's Dark Side," ScienceDaily, March 19, 2012. www.sciencedaily.com.

Girls seem particularly vulnerable on some websites, especially because many bow to pressure to sext or offer titillating information or photos about their lives, only to have such information used against them by cyberbullies. Formats of a few sites, such as ask.fm, qooh.me, and Formspring, allow posters to ask anonymous questions of those with profiles. Many of these questions are explicit, sexually abusive, and misogynistic. As Laura Bates writes in London's *Independent*:

> The anonymity provided by the sites has made them a hotbed for sexual pressure, bullying and abuse. Browsing some of the sites for just a few minutes reveals a torrent of sexual demands, explicit questions and abusive threats to users whose photos suggest they are young teenage girls. Posts included: "You're a fat, ugly, worthless piece of s***. Please kill yourself," "Can we have sex?" and "Wanna do it dirty?"[76]

Vince Mabuza, founder of qooh.me, says about the problem: "Cyber bullying is a huge problem on sites like qooh.me and the others. I have sleepless nights trying to come up with solutions to stop this. [But] shutting the site down won't help, because new ones will be created and the cycle will repeat itself. What we have done is to give users some control by allowing them to disable the anonymous part of the site."[77]

Ending Anonymity

Some people believe that ending the anonymous aspect to the Internet would greatly reduce cyberbullying. They seek government action to disallow websites from providing the ability to post anonymously. As *National Post* columnist Barbara Kay writes, "The teenage years are a difficult passage at best. Social confidence for many teens at this stage of life is notoriously fragile. There seems to be no question but that cyberbullying is one of the most humiliating experiences that can befall a vulnerable teenager. Ending anonymity in such attacks will go far to diminish, if not eliminate this cruelly dark side of social media."[78] Yet others argue that, as in similar cases, ending anonymity will not stop teens and others from creating fictitious profiles, so the situation will not change.

> "There seems to be no question but that cyberbullying is one of the most humiliating experiences that can befall a vulnerable teenager. Ending anonymity in such attacks will go far to diminish, if not eliminate this cruelly dark side of social media."[78]
>
> — *National Post* columnist Barbara Kay.

There are encouraging signs, however, of students standing up for others who are bullied. According to the Pew Research Center, many teens report defending, or seeing others defend, someone being bullied online: 84 percent of people in one Pew study reported seeing other people standing up for a person being harassed online. The same number reported telling the cyberbully to stop the bullying. Also, psychology professor Larry D. Rosen, who studies cyberbullying, reports a surprising observation: Young people can gain virtual empathy, which can foster compassionate and pro-social behavior in the offline world.

In the end, educating teenagers about safe behavior online, monitoring their exposure on the Internet, and taking action at the first sign of a problem may be the only way to prevent cyberbullying. Yet parental involvement can backfire. As an eleven-year-old from Michigan puts it, her cyberbully "kept texting me so many mean things that I wanted to throw my phone against the wall. I told my mom and she called her. After that the mean girls texted me, 'wow you can't fight your own battles!'"[79]

Violent Video Games

Over the past several decades, the video game industry has grown into a huge, multibillion-dollar business. In the most popular games today, violence is a pervasive theme. Moreover, gamers increasingly play online versions with multiple players, and the number of users and hours spent playing has skyrocketed in recent years. In fact, massively multiplayer online games, or MMOs, are the fastest-growing segment of the computer gaming industry. MMOs can support hundreds of thousands of players at the same time.

According to seventeen-year-old Drew, an avid gamer, most games designed for a console such as Xbox also come with the option of playing online with other people: "Most people I know will always opt to play with friends or even random gamers that you've met online. And the violent games are usually the most fun because you really get into it and feel the adrenaline pumping."[80]

> "A wide variety of other factors are more important antecedents of aggression than violent video games."[81]
>
> — David Bond, University of South Florida.

As the games have grown more sophisticated, the violence and the effects of the weapons have become more realistic. Some teens play such games for hours each day, leading some researchers to investigate the possibility of a link between violent video games and violent acts—specifically mass shootings. Researchers have a special interest in shooters who have committed the most horrendous of these acts and have also obsessively played these games. They include:

In December 2012, twenty-year-old Adam Lanza shot and killed his mother, then went to Sandy Hook Elementary School and shot twenty first graders and six staff members. Lanza owned violent video games worth thousands of dollars and a cabinet filled with real weapons.

In July 2012, John Holmes killed twelve people and injured

fifty-eight others in a mass shooting inside a movie theater in Aurora, Colorado, during a midnight screening of the film *The Dark Knight Rises*. Holmes was dressed in tactical clothing and set off tear gas grenades before shooting into the audience with multiple firearms. After searching his apartment, police found multiple violent video games.

Anders Behring Breivik attacked a summer camp on the island of Utøya in Buskerud, Norway, in July 2011, killing 69 campers and injuring 110. Breivik dressed in a homemade police uniform and carried false identification to gain access to the island. After his arrest, Breivik said in court that he played the violent video game *Call of Duty* to improve his hand-eye coordination.

No Evidence of Cause and Effect

Yet even though these shooters possessed and played violent video games, research has yielded no definitive evidence of cause and effect. A 2011 study on the effects of violent video games claimed, "A wide variety of other factors are more important antecedents of aggression than violent video games, including child abuse and neglect, victimization, bullying, drug and alcohol abuse, exposure to violence in the home, neurobiological indicators, low socioeconom-

Gamers wait to test one of the Call of Duty *video games (pictured). Violent video games such as these have a huge following of dedicated players worldwide. Critics say these games may have influenced the actions of people who carried out highly publicized shootings.*

ic status, and access to guns."[81] Lanza, Holmes, and Breivik were all found to be psychologically troubled, and all also had access to guns. Most researchers agree that a mix of factors, not just video games, contribute to mass shootings. In fact, although violent video games have become exceedingly common, no corresponding spike in youth crime has taken place. The number of violent youth offenders fell by more than half between 1994 and 2010, even though video game sales have more than doubled since 1996.

"By providing places for social interaction and relationships beyond the workplace and home, MMOs have the capacity to function much like the hangouts of old."[83]

— Researchers Constance Steinkuehler and Dmitri Williams.

Yet a study in 2012 showed that people who played a violent video game for three days showed increased aggression. Psychologist Brad Bushman, a coauthor of the study, concludes, "Playing video games could be compared to smoking cigarettes. A single cigarette won't cause lung cancer, but smoking over weeks or months or years greatly increases the risk. In the same way, repeated exposure to violent video games may have a cumulative effect on aggression."[82] While many young men play violent video games, few have the urge to kill real people. The positive sides of these games have also been shown. Many researchers have noted that the games promote increased social interaction among peers. Researchers Constance Steinkuehler and Dmitri Williams state, "By providing places for social interaction and relationships beyond the workplace and home, MMOs have the capacity to function much like the hangouts of old." They also say that playing MMOs is not a "single solitary interaction between an individual and a technology but rather, is more akin to playing five-person poker in a neighborhood tavern that is accessible from your own living room." They also found that these virtual gaming places appear "particularly well suited to the formation of bridging social capital—social relationships that, while not usually providing deep emotional support, typically function to expose the individual to a diversity of worldviews."[83]

Explicit Sexual Images

The Internet may also be fostering changes in sexual behavior. In these cases the effects of disinhibition are also at work. A teenage girl would be unlikely to disrobe in front of several boys but may send a partially nude picture of herself to them without understanding that the communication may not be kept private. Such behavior is on the rise. According to March 2011 data from the Council on Communications and Media, 20 percent of teens have sent or posted nude or seminude photos or videos of themselves, and 23 percent think that sexting is fine.

The Internet has also allowed easy access to pornography. According to the organization Internet Safety 101, children in the United States begin viewing hardcore pornography, on average, at age eleven, and four out of five regularly access pornography online. The organization also states that every second, more than twenty-eight thousand Internet users are viewing pornography, and the words *sex* and *porn* rank in the top six most popular search terms. Marriage and family therapist Jill Manning has noted that child or adolescent exposure to Internet pornography can have lasting effects on a child's sexuality, increasing a child's risk of developing aberrant sexual attitudes and addictions.

"Predators are hiding behind the anonymity of the Internet to target kids, to entice kids online—to try to persuade them to meet them in the physical world."[84]

— Ernie Allen, president and CEO of the National Center for Missing and Exploited Children.

While such use is intentional, many children are exposed to pornography purely by accident: Seven out of ten young people have come across pornography by accident while online. For example, 40 percent of youths report that a sexual link popped up after an innocent word search, while 13 percent report being exposed to sexually explicit material when they accidently misspelled a web address. How such exposure will affect behavior is just beginning to be studied. According to Internet Safety 101, youth who look at violent, sexual material are six times more likely to force someone to do something sexual—online or offline—compared with youth with no such exposure. Experts have also warned that viewing pornography is associated with a rise in sexually transmitted diseases and teen pregnancies.

Sexual Predators

The combination of teenage sexual naïveté and overall online anonymity makes the Internet a playground for sexual predators. As Ernie Allen, president and CEO of the National Center for Missing and Exploited Children, says: "Predators are hiding behind

"The Internet is the crime scene of the 21st century, and we must ensure that online video game platforms do not become a digital playground for dangerous predators."[85]

— New York attorney general Eric T. Schneiderman.

the anonymity of the Internet to target kids, to entice kids online—to try to persuade them to meet them in the physical world."[84] The statistics regarding such predation are especially alarming. According to the *Journal of Adolescent Health*, 82 percent of online sex crimes against minors occur after the offender used the victim's social networking site to gain information about the victim. While only 18 percent of young people use chat rooms, the majority of Internet-initiated sex crimes occur on these sites.

The more access children have to the Internet, the more likely it is that they will be approached or victimized by a sexual predator. Internet Safety 101 identifies six risky behaviors, including the percentage of children approached online while using them:

- Fifty percent of children posted personal information.
- Forty-five percent interacted with strangers online.
- Thirty-five percent placed strangers on their buddy lists.
- Twenty-six percent sent personal information to strangers.
- Thirteen percent visited X-rated sites.
- Five percent talked about sex with strangers.

Sexual predators also gain access to children through online games. In New York State alone, the attorney general purged more than thirty-five hundred accounts of registered sex offenders from online gaming sites. According to New York attorney general Eric T. Schneiderman, "The Internet is the crime scene of the 21st century, and we must ensure that online video game platforms do not become a digital playground for dangerous predators."[85]

For Both Good and Ill

The Internet is having a widespread impact on the way people think and how they act. It has allowed people to invade others' privacy and has allowed cruelty and predation to proliferate on an unprecedented scale. Yet people have also used it to connect with and help others and to donate to worthy causes. Used for good or ill, the World Wide Web is a tool that few can decide to opt out of completely.

Facts

- According to 2012 research at Kingston University that examined the behavior of online predators, the conversation between an online offender and a child becomes sexualized within two minutes; if the child does not respond, the predator simply moves on to another child.
- Knowthenet, an online information resource in the United Kingdom, released a 2013 study that reported that 87 percent of teens who reported cyberbullying were targeted on Facebook.
- Multiple surveys report that females are more likely than males to delete their Facebook account after receiving derogatory or otherwise hurtful comments on the site.
- According to the website Internet Safety 101, 68 percent of teens agree that cyberbullying is a major problem for today's young people.
- According to a Cox Communications 2009 Teen Online & Wireless Safety Survey, there are more female cyberbullies than male.
- According to a study at Lancaster University in 2010, four out of five children are unable to determine whether they are talking to an adult posing as a child online.

How Do Online Activities Affect Political and World Events?

Political participation is the hallmark of a robust, well-functioning democracy, and online communication tools have greatly enhanced citizen engagement in the political process in countries throughout the world. In the United States, for example, ordinary citizens are able to put direct pressure on elected officials through e-mails and other personal communication, such as participating in political organizations that solicit directly through online media. Technology has also leveled the playing field because it is inexpensive, decentralized, and interactive, allowing anyone with a computer or access to a library to keep tabs on political figures, interact with them, and influence their decisions.

Technology writer Clay Shirky contends that the Internet has allowed for greater participation in the political process than ever before:

> Since the rise of the Internet in the early 1990s, the world's networked population has grown from the low millions to the low billions. Over the same period, social media have become a fact of life for civil society worldwide, involving many actors—regular citizens, activists, nongovernmental

organizations, telecommunications firms, software providers, governments. . . . As the communications landscape gets denser, more complex, and more participatory, the networked population is gaining greater access to information, more opportunities to engage in public speech, and an enhanced ability to undertake collective action.[86]

Mobilizing Political Action

The Internet has also created a framework to promote a wider and more diverse number of opinions, ideas, and even social movements. Blogs, forums, and discussion boards are now part of an online public sphere that allows for a greater exchange of information to foment political discussion, influence public opinion, and mobilize political action. People no longer rely exclusively on traditional news sources such as television, radio, and newspapers. This massive amount of information and ways to participate in any political discussion, no matter how homespun or narrowly focused, is at the average person's fingertips. Conversely, political candidates, elected officials, and even large corporations use the Internet to keep pace with public discussion and sentiment.

"As the communications landscape gets denser, more complex, and more participatory, the networked population is gaining greater access to information, more opportunities to engage in public speech, and an enhanced ability to undertake collective action."[86]

— Technology writer Clay Shirky.

Facebook is just one example of the new political power of social networking. Facebook users can interact, network, and create a Facebook group to support a political or social cause. A 2012 Canadian study found that such use is becoming more prevalent. Friends are more likely to post and read political messages on each other's Facebook pages and therefore are more likely to respond to calls to action regarding such posts. Many people post a link to a website or to a "vote" button, making it easy for others reading the post to send messages to politicians or organizations working for a particular cause. According to another 2012 study, this one conducted by the University of California–San Diego, a single Facebook message prompted about one-third of a million more people to show up to vote on election day in 2011. The message was a simple reminder to vote, with a button that allowed the viewer to press the "I Voted" button. Friends who saw the social message were more likely to vote. The lead author of the study, James Fowler, says, "Our study suggests that social influence may be the best way to increase voter turnout. Just as importantly, we show that what happens online matters a lot for the 'real world.'"[87]

Others believe the influence of social networking is greatly exaggerated. Although, clearly, political influence may be easier to access, to participate in true change, people must go beyond clicking the "like" button on Facebook. As the website Journalist's Resource puts it: "For those who understand political activism in its pre-digital form—pounding the pavement to distribute printed handouts, door-to-door networking, participating in telephone trees—the notion of 'online activism' can seem an oxymoron. Some observers are concerned about 'slacktivism' or 'clicktivism'—pseudo-activism enabled through quick and easy online actions."[88]

In addition, the argument that people are exposed to a wider variety of opinions and discussion seems to some to be exaggerated. According to a 2010 study in the journal *Perspectives on Politics*, blog readers tend to read only blogs that reinforce their own political beliefs, and few people read blogs on both sides of the political spectrum. A more recent study published in 2013 in the *Journal of Computer-Mediated Communication* found that political talk on Twitter is highly partisan, with users forming separate political groups that reflect their homogeneous views. Furthermore, politically active citizens who use the Internet to communicate, especially young people, are increasingly moving away from neutral news sites to those in line with their own political views.

Building Momentum

Although skeptics find reason to doubt social media's impact on political events, it has clearly provided a very public and expansive forum for people to express their views and inspire action on any number of issues. Just one example occurred in 2010, when the breast cancer organization Susan G. Komen for the Cure announced that it would no longer fund Planned Parenthood because of that group's involvement in abortion. Once announced,

critics of the decision raged across social media, with thousands of messages posted to Komen and Planned Parenthood Facebook pages and advocates rallying support on Twitter. The foundation reversed its decision within days due to the pressure.

Barack Obama was an early adapter of social media. Particularly adept at using Internet technologies to mobilize voters, he is the first president to have held a town hall meeting on Twitter. His use of social media was also key to his 2012 election, say many in the political field. Obama used various online fund-raising tools, including e-mail and the mobile app Quick Donate, to raise $690 million online in 2012. Quick Donate, with more than 1.5 million users, helped Obama raise $115 million. Obama also hired talented technologists to spread his message, and the team helped to revolutionize voter targeting on Facebook. According to the website Mashable, though half of the campaign's target voters aged eighteen

People cast their votes at a New Jersey polling place on Election Day, November 8, 2011. According to a university study, a single Facebook message reminding people to vote prompted about 330,000 people to vote in the 2011 elections.

Jihadist Terrorist Organizations See the Benefit of the Web

Radical jihadists who are loosely affiliated with al Qaeda, the group that carried out the 9/11 terrorist attacks and other attacks worldwide, are taking advantage of the Internet. Many experts believe that the 9/11attacks were planned on the Internet: Computers in Afghanistan belonging to al Qaeda were found to have encrypted messages with information on potential targets in the United States. Al Qaeda groups use the Internet primarily to recruit new members, attract sympathizers, and coordinate operations. They also use the Internet to take responsibility for a terrorist act to increase the visibility of their cause. As the blog *Web Social Impact* contends, "The use of media technologies to spread their message is paramount and the internet is at the moment the ideal arena to accomplish their goal. . . . The terrorist act in itself is worthless without the publicity given by the media."

Ironically, many jihadist websites are located on American servers. The quality of the Internet is higher in the United States, and such organizations are protected by the same free speech rights as others. These rights make the use of the Internet virtually unregulated and make it more difficult for the government to shut down the websites.

Web Social Impact, "Studying Online Terrorism." www.websocialimpact.com.

to twenty-nine were unreachable by phone, 85 percent were friends with an Obama Facebook user. So the campaign used Facebook as a campaign platform, asking supporters to reach out to target voters. Six hundred thousand people reached 5 million voters.

Other political movements are using technologies to gain national support. In 2011 the Occupy Wall Street movement gained momentum using a social networking tool. This one is called a hashtag—a tag embedded in a message posted on Twitter, consisting of a word within the message prefixed with a hash sign (#). The hashtag was posted on Twitter by an activist group called AdBusters on July 13, 2011. It called for protesters to occupy Wall Street on September 17. One day after September 17, tweets about the movement increased 850 percent in twenty-four hours. Protesters flooded Facebook, Twitter, and YouTube to share photos, videos, and their thoughts. Mainstream media largely ignored the burgeoning movement, mostly because it seemed to lack an organized cause.

Media attention grew with the group's increasingly visible presence on social media sites, however. Starting on Wall Street in New York City, Occupy movements expanded across the country in many large cities, all fueled by social networking sites. Cities that tried to eject the protesters by force were quickly condemned on social networking sites. The day-to-day activities of the protesters, and the police and National Guard attempts to eject them, began to appear in national newspapers with regularity. National figures such as Obama and former House Speaker Newt Gingrich commented on the movement's goals, saying that it clearly was expressing the frustration felt by thousands of out-of-work and disgruntled Americans.

Speaking Out

While Occupy Wall Street protested national economic policy, a far different protest focused on a single issue. In 2012 American fast-food chain Chick-fil-A became the target of protest after chief operating officer Dan Cathy went public with comments opposing same-sex marriage. This followed news reports that Chick-fil-A's charitable endeavor, the S. Truett Cathy family–operated WinShape Foundation, had contributed millions of dollars to political organizations that opposed gay rights. Gay rights activists called for protests and boycotts of the chain while counterprotesters voiced support—all by using Facebook.

Garnering support for an organized same-sex Kiss Day at Chick-fil-As, gay rights activists asked same-sex couples to show up at the restaurants to kiss in protest and post videos or photos of the event. Those in support of the Chick-fil-A stance also used

Facebook to ask people to show up on the same day to "show Chick-fil-A thanks for their support of Love, Equality, and the Real Definition of Marriage!"[89] Many of the restaurants across the country were deluged at the appointed time on the day of the protest. After the event, Chick-fil-A released a statement that read, "Going forward, our intent is to leave the policy debate over same-sex marriage to the government and political arena,"[90] clearly wishing not to gain national attention for its political views again.

The public is not alone in catching on to the use of social networking tools. The Bureau of Land Management (BLM), responsible for many public lands across the United States, is using the popular cycling app STRAVA. On STRAVA, cyclists can post what trails they rode and compare notes with other riders. The BLM now looks at the site to keep tabs on, close down, and prevent cyclists from using such trails. Says cyclist Morgan Harris, "Cyclists are unintentionally undermining their own cause by using Strava."[91]

Social Networking and Repressive Regimes

While social networking has made an impact within the democratic United States, it is also allowing for change in countries with repressive regimes. Citizens in Tunisia, Iran, and Egypt used social networking to organize protests and communicate their intentions to the world in 2011. In Egypt in 2011 citizen protesters (with backing from the military) ousted longtime dictator Hosni Mubarak. One of the key figures in the protests, Wael Ghonim, directly credits Facebook with his and other protesters' ability to keep the revolutionary movement going and to keep it in the public eye:

> I want to meet Mark Zuckerberg one day and thank him. . . . I'm talking on behalf of Egypt. . . . This revolution started online. This revolution started on Facebook. This revolution started . . . in June 2010 when hundreds of thousands of Egyptians started collaborating content. We would post a video on Facebook that would be shared by 60,000 people on their walls within a few hours. I've always said that if you want to liberate a society just give them the Internet.[92]

The power of the Internet might also be working for, not just against, repressive regimes. Some of these governments are also beginning to understand the power of social media and are learning to manipulate these sites to reinforce their power. Some commentators believe that social media platforms can become tools of repression. Governments have cut off access to the Internet and other social media to prevent subversive protests and communications. The Egyptian government cut off Internet access during the 2011 protests, although the action did not prevent the toppling of that regime. The Chinese shut down Internet access to Xinjiang Province for six months to prevent Muslim protests there in 2009. Pakistan blocked access to YouTube in 2009.

Other governments are using the Internet to advertise their own agendas. In her book *Consent of the Networked*, author Rebecca MacKinnon writes that the Chinese government has co-opted online social media sites to monitor online discussions. Using the information gathered, Chinese officials have shut down sites that do

Egyptians celebrate the resignation of president Hosni Mubarak in 2011. With the help of social networking sites, Egyptians organized protests and communicated their intentions to the world in 2011.

not conform to the government message, while at the same time planting users to direct discussions toward a pro-government stance.

Flash Mob Protests

Twitter is also a catalyst for bringing together citizens reacting to financial crises, policy decisions, and other political events. When European countries were in financial crisis because of the falling value of the euro, young people in Madrid, Spain, used Twitter to organize a flash mob to spur protests. According to the consulting firm Accenture:

> "Digital citizens can make an impact at lightning-fast pace, and they will come to expect the same of government."[93]
>
> — Accenture, a managing consulting firm.

> Digital citizens can make an impact at lightning-fast pace, and they will come to expect the same of government. In 2011 thousands of young people in Spain protested against mass unemployment, austerity measures and political corruption. The movement started as a flash mob in Puerta del Sol in Madrid on May 15, 2011 and spread quickly. Election turnout just days later was significantly affected. The ruling socialists suffered their worst electoral defeat in more than 30 years.[93]

Promoting Change

In 2012 one of the most viral videos of all time demonstrated the role of social media in driving social change. Filmmaker Jason Russell used the power of the Internet to create international recognition of African cult and militia leader and indicted war criminal Joseph Kony. Kony was convicted by the International Criminal Court in the Hague in 2005 for his role in the torture and murder of African civilians. *Kony 2012* (officially *KONY 2012* or *Kony2012*) is a short film created by the nongovernmental organization Invisible Children. The film's purpose was to promote the charity's Stop Kony movement. The film depicted Kony's brutal tactics and his kidnapping and consignment of young children, whom he arms and trains to fight for his army. The film, which was posted on YouTube, received intense exposure.

Pressure on international governments led the United States

The Perils of Wide-Reaching Connectivity

David E. Hoffman is a Pulitzer Prize–winning author and a contributing editor to *Foreign Policy*. Hoffman believes that the digital revolution has been a powerful liberating force for millions of people around the globe, but he notes some of the dangers associated with a connected world:

> We live in an age of person-to-person communications that are more fluid and accessible than at any time in human history. We routinely search across oceans of data in a fraction of a second. And you can hold a device to do this in the palm of your hand. But there are danger signs. The world is now totally dependent on connectivity. Finance, medicine, education, science, news, national security and culture are all reliant on networks. What if the power in a major American city is abruptly switched off by a single command from a remote server that no one can trace? Or a dam sabotaged? Or the wrong signal causing stock markets to crash? Computers have been such an impressive force for good that it may be hard to think about the underside, about an arms race in cyberspace, but it is plausible. The United States, China, Russia and others are now investing in offensive cyber weapons, and doing it largely in secret, without public debate.

David E. Hoffman, "Class Act," *Foreign Policy*, May 25, 2012. http://hoffman.foreignpolicy.com.

to spearhead congressional action to help the Ugandan military capture Kony. In 2011 Obama authorized the deployment of approximately one hundred combat-equipped US troops to central

Africa. In April 2013 the Obama administration offered up to $5 million in rewards for information leading to the capture of Kony. While Kony remains at large, *Kony 2012* shows the critical role social media plays as a news source, especially for people under age thirty. Says Patricia Vanderbilt of the *Huffington Post*:

> I commend the filmmakers at Invisible Children Inc. for making a video that in one week has resoundingly achieved its objective: it has made Joseph Kony famous. Millions who watched the video learned about the decades-long conflict in Uganda for the first time. The slogan "Stop Kony" is a great catchphrase to be hashtagged around the twitter-verse, and the awareness that spreads with it is undoubtedly valuable. That the video has over 70 million views is a testament to the power and potential of social media to promote dialogue and—one hopes—positive change.[94]

"That the [Kony] video has over 70 million views is a testament to the power and potential of social media to promote dialogue and—one hopes—positive change."[94]

— Journalist Patricia Vanderbilt.

Still, skeptics say that even though *Kony 2012* brought media attention to a problem, it is unclear how people should view its overall success. For one thing, Kony is still at large. In addition, some critics argue that political policy should not be determined by the popularity of a YouTube video. They worry that Obama's response may have been more about currying public favor than coming up with a thoughtful plan of action for one of the world's many problems. Finally, some analysts argue that people may be easily manipulated by sound bites on social media, leaving those who are good at manipulating that medium with more power than they deserve or should have. As web developer Anthony Wing Kosner comments:

> The fact is that social media has changed the world, but perhaps in more superficial ways than we first assume. Far from leveling all hierarchy, it just shifts it around some. Joseph Kony is so manifestly evil because he commits crimes of hierarchy: forcing the child to kill the parent, making children soldiers and sex slaves. . . . But in this new global

social media hierarchy, it is still these American practitioners that are calling the shots.[95]

For Good or Ill?

The online news source WikiLeaks has created similar controversy over whether its ability to release classified information constitutes a boon or a bane to the public. WikiLeaks is a nonprofit media group that claims to "publish material of ethical, political and historical significance providing a universal way for the revealing of suppressed and censored injustices."[96] It has come under fire, especially after its November 2012 release of classified military information. WikiLeaks founder Julian Assange faces charges brought by the US government for espionage, as does the supplier of the information, Bradley Manning. While traditional news outlets have been banned from some war zones and from publishing articles on particular news stories, WikiLeaks continues to publish information critical of nations such as the United States. Says Steve Myers, managing editor of Poynter Online: "Wikileaks has shifted power away from the monoliths that once determined what is news and toward the people who, before the Web, would have been stopped in the newspaper lobby before they could see a reporter."[97]

"WikiLeaks has shifted power away from the monoliths that once determined what is news and toward the people who, before the Web, would have been stopped in the newspaper lobby before they could see a reporter."[97]

— Steve Myers, managing editor of Poynter Online.

The debate over whether WikiLeaks is a positive force in international media may be moot when every citizen has a cell phone and is able to post video of live news events seconds after they happen. The Abu Ghraib prisoner scandal of 2004 was initially broken to the media when images of US soldiers torturing prisoners, taken with small digital cameras or cell phone cameras by the soldiers, were downloaded directly into computer files or e-mails. These images were sent instantly to an international audience of friends, colleagues, and, ultimately, news organizations. Whether such a scandal would have been reported eventually is almost beside the point. A citizen media, uncensored and with a ready method of publication, is a genie that cannot be put back in the bottle.

Facts

- According to Joseph Kahne, chair of the MacArthur Foundation's Research Network on Youth and Participatory Politics, 41 percent of young people surveyed reported engaging in political activity on social media, such as tweeting support for a political cause or forwarding political information via Facebook.

- Citizen journalists have used online networking tools to break important news stories, such as the report that the Recovery.gov website listing federal stimulus money was fraught with errors and that $6.4 billion in stimulus funds were awarded to more than four hundred nonexistent congressional districts.

- The web group Peace on Facebook uses technology to enable people from diverse political and religious backgrounds to connect with one another.

- Twitter, Facebook, and many smartphone applications are the new tools used by governments to alert victims and relief workers when disasters strike or public health concerns emerge.

- Social media has made it difficult for governments to control news of political deaths, military coups, and other political events; when Libyan leader Muammar Gaddafi was shot during a coup in 2011, footage captured on an iPhone showing his corpse was widely circulated via the Internet and social media.

Source Notes

Introduction: The Fear of Invention

1. Richard Conniff, "What the Luddites Really Fought Against," *Smithsonian*, March 2011. www.smithsonianmag.com.
2. Quoted in Vaughan Bell, "Don't Touch That Dial! A History of Media Technology Scares, from the Printing Press to Facebook," *Slate*, February 15, 2010. www.slate .com.
3. Quoted in Bell, "Don't Touch That Dial! A History of Media Technology Scares, from the Printing Press to Facebook."
4. Tony Dokoupil, "Is the Web Driving Us Mad?," Daily Beast, July 9, 2012. www .dailybeast.com.
5. Quoted in Conniff, "What the Luddites Really Fought Against."

Chapter One: What Led to the Debate Over How Online Activities Affect Society?

6. William Davidow, *Overconnected: The Promise and Threat of the Internet*. Harrison, NY: Delphinium, 2011, p. 7.
7. Davidow, *Overconnected*, p. 7.
8. Jeffrey Rosen, "Your Blog or Mine?," *New York Times*, December 19, 2004. www .nytimes.com.
9. Quoted in Francesca Davis DiPiazza, *Friend Me: 600 Years of Social Networking in America*. Minneapolis: Twenty-First Century, 2012, p. 87.
10. Quoted in DiPiazza, *Friend Me*, p. 87.
11. Marcia Clemmitt, "Social Media Explosion," *CQ Researcher*, January 25, 2013. http://library.cqpress.com.
12. Quoted in DiPiazza, *Friend Me*, p. 89.
13. Quoted in Mark Johnson, "Thc History of Twitter," Socialnomics, January 23, 2013. www.socialnomics.net.
14. Quoted in NBC News, "Tweet to Earth: 'Launch Was Awesome!!,'' May 13, 2009. www.nbcnews.com.
15. NASA, "NASA Extends the World Wide Web Out into Space," January 22, 2010. www.nasa.gov.
16. Quoted in Jeff Zeleny, "Obama Digs In for His BlackBerry," *New York Times*, January 7, 2009. www.nytimes.com.
17. Larry D. Rosen, *iDisorder: Understanding Our Obsession with Technology and Overcoming Its Hold on Us*. New York: Palgrave Macmillan, 2012, p. 9.
18. Davidow, *Overconnected*, p. 136.
19. Clay A. Johnson, *The Information Diet: A Case for Conscious Consumption*. Sebastopol, CA: O'Reilly, 2012, p. 4.

20. Quoted in Nicholas Carr, *The Shallows: What the Internet Is Doing to Our Brains.* New York: Norton, 2011, p. 6.

21. *Wikipedia*, "*Wikipedia*: Ten Things You May Not Know About *Wikipedia*," May 1, 2013. http://en.wikipedia.org.

22. Quoted in Joann Pan, "Map the Pounds of Bacteria Living on Your Body," Mashable, December 14, 2012. mashable.com.

23. Davidow, *Overconnected*, p. 157.

24. Nicholas Carr, "Is Google Making Us Stupid?," *Atlantic*, July/August 2008. www.theatlantic.com.

25. Quoted in Carr, *The Shallows*, p. 7.

26. Quoted in Carr, *The Shallows*, p. 7.

27. Michael J. Rosenfeld, "Searching for a Mate: The Rise of the Internet as a Social Intermediary," *American Sociological Review*, 2012. www.asanet.org.

28. Johnson, *The Information Diet*, p. 145.

Chapter Two: How Do Online Activities Affect Youth?

29. Hanna Rosin, "The Touch-Screen Generation," *Atlantic*, March 20, 2013. www.theatlantic.com.

30. Interview with the author, April 2013.

31. Dokoupil, "Is the Web Driving Us Mad?"

32. Quoted in Matt Richtel, "Digitally Aided Education, Using the Student's Own Electronic Gear," *New York Times*, March 22, 2013. www.nytimes.com.

33. Quoted in University of Oxford, "UK Teenagers Without the Internet Are 'Educationally Disadvantaged,'" December 22, 2012. www.ox.ac.uk.

34. Quoted in Stacey Kennelly, "The Good and Bad of Online Education," *Chico News & Review*, August 19, 2010. www.newsreview.com.

35. Mark Edmundson, "The Trouble with Online Education," *New York Times*, July 19, 2012. www.nytimes.com.

36. Quoted in Kennelly, "The Good and Bad of Online Education."

37. Rosin, "The Touch-Screen Generation."

38. Jonah Lehrer, "Is Google Ruining Your Memory?," *Wired*, July 15, 2011. www.wired.com.

39. Lehrer, "Is Google Ruining Your Memory?"

40. Maia Szalavitz, "Does the Internet Really Make Everyone Crazy?," *Time*, July 13, 2012. http://healthland.time.com.

41. Rosen, *iDisorder*, p. 33.

42. Quoted in Rosen, *iDisorder*, p. 14.

43. Rosen, *iDisorder*, p. 10.

44. Quoted in Johah Lehrer, "Is Facebook Ruining Human Friendships?," *Wired*, November 8, 2010. www.wired.com.

45. Alice Marwick and danah boyd, "Teens Text More than Adults, but They're Still Just Teens," Daily Beast, May 20, 2012. www.thedailybeast.com.

46. Dokoupil, "Is the Web Driving Us Mad?"

47. Quoted in ScienceDaily, "Pathological Internet Use Among Teens May Lead to Depression," August 3, 2010. www.sciencedaily.com.

48. Dokoupil, "Is the Web Driving Us Mad?"

49. Quoted in ScienceDaily, "Facebook Makes Us Feel Good About Ourselves, Research Finds," June 26, 2012. www.sciencedaily.com.

Chapter Three: Are Online Activities Addictive?

50. Dave Mosher, "High Wired: Does Addictive Internet Use Restructure the Brain?," *Scientific American*, June 17, 2011. www.scientificamerican.com.
51. Quoted in Ned Hepburn, "Life in the Age of Internet Addiction," *Week*, January 24, 2013. http://theweek.com.
52. Johnson, *The Information Diet*, p. 51.
53. Carr, *The Shallows*, p. 16.
54. Quoted in Carr, *The Shallows*, p. 120.
55. Dokoupil, "Is the Web Driving Us Mad?"
56. Peter Gray, "Video Game Addiction: Does It Occur? If So, Why?," *Psychology Today*, February 2, 2012. www.psychologytoday.com.
57. Quoted in Hepburn, "Life in the Age of Internet Addiction."
58. Quoted in Mosher, "High Wired."
59. Gray, "Video Game Addiction."
60. Quoted in Sherry Rauh, "Video Game Addiction No Fun," WebMD, 2006. www.webmd.com.
61. Quoted in ScienceDaily, "Are You a Facebook Addict?," May 7, 2012. www.sciencedaily.com.
62. Quoted in Emmanuel Samoglou, "Do You Have a Tweeting Disorder?," *Canadian Business*, September 22, 2011. www.canadianbusiness.com.
63. Erin Biba, "Facebook: Personal Branding Made Easy," *Wired*, June 19, 2011. www.wired.com.
64. Hanna Krasnova et al., "Envy on Facebook: A Hidden Threat to Users' Life Satisfaction?," 11th International Conference on Wirtschaftsinformatik, 2013. http://warhol.wiwi.hu-berlin.de.
65. Quoted in ScienceDaily, "Are Social Networking Internet Sites a Factor in Psychotic Symptoms?," November 20, 2012. www.sciencedaily.com.
66. Quoted in ScienceDaily, "Are Social Networking Internet Sites a Factor in Psychotic Symptoms?"

Chapter Four: Do Online Activities Promote Antisocial Behavior?

67. Quoted in Mark Di Ionno, "Exclusive Interview with Dharun Ravi: 'I'm Very Sorry About Tyler,'" *New Jersey Star-Ledger*, March 22, 2012.
68. John Suler, "The Online Disinhibition Effect," *CyberPsychology and Behavior*, 2004. http://users.rider.edu.
69. Suler, "The Online Disinhibition Effect."
70. Suler, "The Online Disinhibition Effect."
71. Suler, "The Online Disinhibition Effect."
72. OvercomeBullying.org, "Cyber Bullying," 2011. www.overcomebullying.org.
73. Quoted in Steve Pokin, "'My Space' Hoax Ends with Suicide of Dardenne Prairie Teen," *St. Louis (MO) Post-Dispatch*, November 11, 2007. www.stltoday.com.
74. OvercomeBullying.org, "Cyber Bullying."
75. Kelly McParland, "Bullying Is an Evil on the Same Level as Sexual Abuse and Deserves a Similar Response," *National Post* (Toronto), October 15, 2012. http://news.nationalpost.com.

76. Laura Bates, "Next Generation of Social Media 'Exposing Girls to Sexual Abuse,'" *Independent* (London), February 13, 2013. www.independent.co.uk.
77. Quoted in Bates, "Next Generation of Social Media 'Exposing Girls to Sexual Abuse.'"
78. Barbara Kay, "Amanda Todd's Death Shows the Need to Expose Cyberbullies," *National Post* (Toronto), October 12, 2012. http://fullcomment.nationalpost.com.
79. Quoted in Sameer Hinduja and Justin Patchin, "Fact Sheet: Cyberbullying Identification, Prevention, and Response," Cyberbullying Research Center, June 14, 2011. http://cyberbullying.us.
80. Interview with the author, March 18, 2013.
81. David Bond, "The Effects of Violent Video Games on Aggressive Behavior and the Relationship to School Shootings," University of South Florida Scholar Commons, April 1, 2011.
82. Quoted in Rick Nauert, "Negative Effects of Violent Video Games May Build over Time," Psych Central, December 2012. http://psychcentral.com.
83. Quoted in Rick Nauert, "Online Video Games Socially Helpful?," Psych Central, August 17, 2006. http://psychcentral.com.
84. Quoted in Internet Safety 101, "Predators' Access to Kids." www.internetsafety101.org.
85. Quoted in James Brightman, "NY Attorney General Purges Another 2,100 Sex Offenders from Online Gaming," GamesIndustry International, December 19, 2012. www.gamesindustry.biz.

Chapter Five: How Do Online Activies Affect Political and World Events?

86. Clay Shirky, "The Political Power of Social Media," *Foreign Affairs*, January/February 2011. www.foreignaffairs.com.
87. Quoted in Inga Kiderra, "Facebook Boosts Voter Turnout," UC San Diego News Center, September 12, 2012. http://ucsdnews.ucsd.edu.
88. Journalist's Resource, "Digital Activism and Organizing: Research Review and Reading List," March 12, 2013. http://journalistsresource.org.
89. Quoted in CNN, "Gay Rights Activists to Hold Kiss Protests at Chick-fil-A Restaurants," August 2, 2012. www.cnn.com.
90. Quoted in *USA Today*, "Chick-fil-A Exec Takes Stance Against Same-Sex Marriage," July 19, 2012. http://usatoday.com.
91. Interview with the author, April 12, 2013.
92. Quoted in Catharine Smith, "Egypt's Facebook Revolution: Wael Ghonim Thanks the Social Network," *Huffington Post*, November 30, 2011. www.huffingtonpost.com.
93. Accenture, "How Social Media Is Reinventing Government," 2012. www.accenture.com.
94. Patricia Vanderbilt, "*Kony 2012*: Anatomy of a Social Media Sensation," *Huffington Post*, March 14, 2012. www.huffingtonpost.com.
95. Anthony Wing Kosner, "12 Lessons from *KONY 2012* from Social Media Power Users," *Forbes*, March 9, 2012. www.forbes.com.
96. Quoted in Seth Liss, "WikiLeaks Takes Social Media to Another Level," *Fort Lauderdale (FL) Sun Sentinel*, January 7, 2011. http://articles.sun-sentinel.com.
97. Quoted in Liss, "WikiLeaks Takes Social Media to Another Level."

Related Organizations and Websites

American Library Association (ALA)

50 E. Huron St.
Chicago, IL 60611
phone: (800) 545-2433
fax: (312) 440-9374
e-mail: ala@ala.org
website: www.ala.org

The ALA was founded in 1876 to provide leadership for the development, promotion, and improvement of library and information services and to ensure access to information for all. It is opposed to censorship in all forms. The association's website provides information about legislation that affects Internet access at public libraries.

Berkman Center for Internet & Society

Harvard University
23 Everett St., 2nd Floor
Cambridge, MA 02138
phone: (617) 495-7547
fax: (617) 495-7641
e-mail: cyber@law.harvard.edu
website: http://cyber.law.harvard.edu

The Berkman Center for Internet & Society was founded in 1997 to explore and understand cyberspace and help pioneer its development. To this end, the center conducts research on a wide variety of issues related to the Internet, including privacy, politics, law, and culture. Many publications are available on the center's website, including the 2010 report *Youth, Privacy, and Reputation*.

Center for Democracy and Technology (CDT)

1634 I St. NW, Suite 1100
Washington, DC 20006
phone: (202) 637-9800
fax: (202) 637-0968
e-mail: info@cdt.org
website: www.cdt.org

The CDT is a nonprofit civil liberties organization dedicated to keeping the Internet and all new communications media open, innovative, and free. The CDT works to promote its goals through research and education. Publications available on the website include press releases, position statements, and numerous reports related to free expression.

Center for Safe and Responsible Internet Use

474 W. 29th Ave.
Eugene, OR 97405
phone: (541) 556-1145
e-mail: contact@csriu.org
website: www.cyberbully.org

The Center for Safe and Responsible Internet Use was founded by Nancy Willard, an expert on student use of the Internet. The center offers numerous reports and guides designed to address the challenges related to managing web technologies in the schools. Its new program, Embracing Digital Youth, seeks to ensure that all young people become "cybersavvy" as they learn to navigate the digital world.

Electronic Frontier Foundation (EFF)

454 Shotwell St.
San Francisco, CA 94110-1914
phone: (415) 436-9333
e-mail: information@eff.org
website: www.eff.org

The EFF is an organization of students, lawyers, policy analysts, and others who seek to foster awareness of telecommunications issues as they relate to civil liberties, including the right to free speech and privacy in the digital world. The group brings and defends lawsuits to preserve First Amendment rights in all telecommunications technologies.

Electronic Privacy Information Center (EPIC)

1718 Connecticut Ave. NW, Suite 200
Washington, DC 20009
phone: (202) 483-1140
fax: (202) 483-1248
website: http://epic.org

EPIC is a research center founded in 1994 to focus public attention on civil liberty issues involving the Internet and emerging digital technologies. The website offers news and information on a variety of topics, including children's online privacy, social networking, and Facebook.

Federal Trade Commission (FTC)

600 Pennsylvania Ave. NW
Washington, DC 20580
phone: (202) 326-2222
website: www.ftc.gov

The FTC is the consumer protection agency of the federal government. It deals with many issues that pertain to economics, including unfair and illegal business practices and identity theft on the Internet. Its website includes numerous publications about how to safely use the Internet and digital technologies.

Focus on the Family

8605 Explorer Dr.
Colorado Springs, CO 80920
phone: (800) 232-6459
website: www.family.org

Focus on the Family is a global Christian ministry dedicated to helping families thrive while preserving biblical beliefs. To this end, the organization provides numerous guidelines on topics such as parenting, relationships, marriage, and social issues. The project Focus on Your Child provides instructive materials to help parents address issues associated with social networking and Internet safety.

GetNetWise

e-mail: cmatsuda@neted.org
website: www.getnetwise.org

GetNetWise is a public service coalition provided by Internet industry corporations and public interest organizations to help ensure that Internet users have safe online experiences. The website offers articles on many topics, including online child safety, privacy, and social networking.

Internet Education Foundation (IEF)

Center for Democracy and Technology
1634 I St. NW, Suite 1100
Washington, DC 20006
phone: (202) 638-4370
fax: (202) 637-0968
e-mail: tim@neted.org
website: www.neted.org

The IEF is a nonprofit organization founded in 1996 that supports privacy, free expression, and other civil liberties as they relate to the Internet. To this end, the foundation works to inform policy making on Internet-related issues both in government and the private sector. It also seeks to educate the public about the challenges presented by the Internet and to offer solutions.

Internet Society (ISOC)

1775 Wiehle Ave., Suite 201
Reston, VA 20190-5108
phone: (703) 439-2120
fax: (703) 326-9881
e-mail: isoc@isoc.org
website: ww.isoc.org

The ISOC is an international, nonprofit group founded in 1992 to provide leadership in the formation of Internet-related standards, education, and public policy. Its goal is to ensure the open development of the Internet for the benefit of people throughout the world. The ISOC acts as a global clearinghouse for Internet information and educational materials.

Wired Safety

e-mail: webmaster@wiredsafety.org
website: www.wiredsafety.org

Wired Safety is a nonprofit group founded in 1995 to promote online safety and education. The group has more than nine thousand volunteers who operate online to provide help and resources to victims of cybercrime and harassment. Wired Safety provides extensive information on all aspects of cyberspace safety, privacy, and security issues.

Additional Reading

Books

Joel Brenner, *America the Vulnerable: Inside the New Threat Matrix of Digital Espionage, Crime, and Warfare*. New York: Penguin, 2011.

Brian X. Chen, *Always On: How the iPhone Unlocked the Anything-Anytime-Anywhere Future—and Locked Us In*. Cambridge, MA: Da Capo, 2011.

Clay A. Johnson, *The Information Diet: A Case for Conscious Consumption*. Sebastopol, CA: O'Reilly, 2012.

Andrew Keen, *Digital Vertigo: How Today's Online Social Revolution Is Dividing, Diminishing, and Disorienting Us*. New York: St. Martin's, 2012.

Evgeny Morozov, *To Save Everything, Click Here*. New York: Public Affairs, 2013.

Eric Schmidt and Jared Cohen, *The New Digital Age: Reshaping the Future of People, Nations and Business*. New York: Knopf, 2013.

Clay Shirky, *Cognitive Surplus: Creativity and Generosity in a Connected Age*. New York: Penguin, 2010.

Sherry Turkle, *Alone Together: Why We Expect More from Technology and Less from Each Other*. New York: Basic Books, 2011.

Richard Watson, *Future Minds: How the Digital Age Is Changing Our Minds, Why This Matters, and What We Can Do About It*. Boston: Brealey, 2010.

Periodicals and Internet Sources

Marcia Clemmit, "Social Media Explosion," *CQ Researcher*, January 25, 2013.

Sandra Cortesi and Urs Gasser, "Parents, Teens, and Online Privacy," Berkman Center for Internet & Society, November 20, 2012. http://cyber.law.harvard.edu/node/8053.

Mark Johnson, "The History of Twitter," Socialnomics, January 23, 2013. http://www.socialnomics.net/2013/01/23/the-history-of-twitter/.

Scott Kleinberg, "Online Privacy Settings Apply Offline Too," *Chicago Tribune*, April 12, 2012.

Drew Olanoff, "Twitter's Social Impact Can't Be Measured, but It's the Pulse of the Planet," TechCrunch, January 15, 2013. http://techcrunch.com/2013/01/15/twitters-social-impact-cant-be-measured-but-its-the-pulse-of-the-planet/.

Larry D. Rosen, "The Power of Like: We Like Being Liked . . . on Facebook," *Psychology Today*, July 15, 2012.

Somini Sengupta, "Letting Down Our Guard with Web Privacy," *New York Times*, March 30, 2013.

Ryan Tate, "Social Media Is Eating Our Lives (and Pinterest Is Chewing Fastest)," *Wired*, December 3, 2012.

Craig Timberg, "A World Away from Facebook," *Washington Post*, August 5, 2012.

Catalin Zorzine, "The State of Social Sharing in 2013," *Wired*, April 15, 2013.

Index

Note: Boldface page numbers indicate illustrations.

About the Authors

Bonnie Szumski has been an editor and author of nonfiction books for twenty-five years. Jill Karson has been an editor and author of nonfiction books for young adults for fifteen years.